Marshall Brian

WELLSPRING OF GUIDANCE

Erratum

Riḍván Message 1965, page 64, line 28, . . .
"Urgent . . ." should read "Unique . . ."

Wellspring of Guidance

Wherever a Bahá'í community exists, whether large or small, let it be distinguished for its abiding sense of security and faith, its high standard of rectitude, its complete freedom from all forms of prejudice, the spirit of love among its members, and for the closely knit fabric of its social life.

The Universal House of Justice

MESSAGES 1963-1968

The Universal House of Justice

1970

BAHÁ'Í PUBLISHING TRUST · WILMETTE, ILLINOIS

Copyright © 1969 by the National Spiritual Assembly
of the Bahá'ís of the United States of America

All rights reserved
Printed in the United States of America

Second Printing 1970

Standard Book Number: 0–87743–032–2

Preface

On April 21, 1963, the momentous first International Bahá'í Convention yielded the long-awaited crown of the Bahá'í Administrative Order: the Universal House of Justice. This institution came into being at an unprecedented landmark in Bahá'í history known as the Most Great Jubilee, which, all at once, displayed the rich harvest of the Ten Year World Crusade inaugurated by the beloved Guardian of the Cause of God, Shoghi Effendi, in 1953; brought to an auspicious conclusion at the Bahá'í World Congress in London the dynamic ninth part of the spiritual evolution of man that began with the Adamic Cycle; and ushered mankind to the threshold of the tenth part of that divine process destined to culminate in the Christ-promised Kingdom of God on earth.

Although the Guardian had passed away at the midway point of the Ten Year Crusade, the Bahá'ís executed with unflagging determination the goals of the Crusade in keeping with his explicit instructions. The Hands of the Cause of God, the "Chief Stewards of Bahá'u'lláh's embryonic World Commonwealth," impelled by the impending necessity to restore unerring guidance to the day-to-day affairs of the swelling Bahá'í community, called for the election of the supreme legislative institution of the Faith as set forth in the Will and Testament of 'Abdu'l-Bahá.

Ever since its first reassuring message to the believers from the platform of the Jubilee celebration in London, the Universal House of Justice has been communicating its guidance to the Bahá'í world through letters and cablegrams. This volume contains major messages from April 1963 through October 1968, six months following the second election of the Universal House of Justice. Except for eight, these messages are addressed to all national spiritual assemblies or to the Bahá'ís of the world, in such terms as "Bahá'ís of the East and West," "Followers of Bahá'u'lláh throughout the world," etc. Those addressed to the national spiritual assemblies are marked by an asterisk (*) beside each date.

Three messages are addressed to conferences; two to the Bahá'í youth in every land; one to a specific national spiritual assembly; and two to an individual believer. The latter three have been made available to the Bahá'ís throughout the world by special permission of the Universal House of Justice.

These messages enunciate the Nine Year Plan, analyze its progress, and reflect the attention the Universal House of Justice has given to the development of the institutions of the Faith and individual believers to better equip them for the worldwide tasks of the Nine Year Plan.

NATIONAL SPIRITUAL ASSEMBLY
BAHÁ'ÍS OF THE UNITED STATES

[The titles and subtitles of messages other than those entitled "Teaching the Masses" and "Universal Participation" do not form part of the original messages.]

Contents

Preface v
First Statement from the Universal House of Justice 1
Message to National Conventions—1963 4
Seat of the Universal House of Justice; New Arrangements for Pilgrims 9
The Guardianship 11
Second World-Encircling Enterprise 12
A Service Every Believer Can Render 19
Call to Action—Nine Year Plan 22
Dedication of the Mother Temple of Europe 28
Teaching the Masses 31
Universal Participation 37
Development of the Institution of the Hands of the Cause of God 40
Unassailable Foundation of the Cause of God 44
Majestic Process Gathering Momentum 57
Call for Pioneers 68
Observance of Bahá'í Holy Days 69
Arming for Third Phase of the Nine Year Plan 71
The Guardianship and the Universal House of Justice 81
Unique Opportunity in Human History (Letter to Bahá'í Youth) 92
Three More National Assemblies to be Formed Riḍván 1967 98
Vital Needs of the Bahá'í World Center 99
Worldwide Proclamation—A New Dimension 102
One Hundred Fiftieth Anniversary of Birth of Bahá'u'lláh 116

Nature and Purpose of Proclamation 117
The Time is Ripe (Message to the Six Intercontinental Conferences) 119
Third Phase of Nine Year Plan Begins 122
Significant Step at United Nations 123
The Paramount Goal of Teaching 124
Convocation of First Oceanic Conference 130
Relationship of Bahá'ís to Politics 131
Newly Elected Universal House of Justice 137
Message to National Conventions—1968 138
Continental Boards of Counselors Established 139
Appointment of Continental Boards of Counselors 140
From Gallipoli to the Most Great Prison (Message to First Oceanic Conference) 145
All May Share Laurels of Accomplishment 150
Pathway of Service for Bahá'í Youth in Every Land 152
In Memoriam
  Ioas, Leroy 157
  Grossmann, Hermann 157
  Ḥakím, Luṭfu'lláh 158
  Samandarí, Ṭarázu'lláh 158

WELLSPRING OF GUIDANCE

First Statement from the Universal House of Justice

[*Presented April 30, 1963, at the World Congress*]

"All praise, O my God, be to Thee Who art the Source of all glory and majesty, of greatness and honor, of sovereignty and dominion, of loftiness and grace, of awe and power. Whomsoever Thou willest Thou causest to draw nigh unto the Most Great Ocean, and on whomsoever Thou desirest Thou conferrest the honor of recognizing Thy Most Ancient Name. Of all who are in heaven and on earth, none can withstand the operation of Thy sovereign Will. From all eternity Thou didst rule the entire creation, and Thou wilt continue for evermore to exercise Thy dominion over all created things. There is none other God but Thee, the Almighty, the Most Exalted, the All-Powerful, the All-Wise."

Beloved friends:

On this glorious occasion, the celebration of the Most Great Jubilee, we raise our grateful thanks to Bahá'u'lláh for all His bounties showered upon the friends throughout the world. This historic moment marks at one and the same time the fulfillment of Daniel's prophecy, the hundredth anniversary of the Declaration of the Promised One of all ages, the termination of the first epoch of the Divine Plan of 'Abdu'l-Bahá designed to establish the Faith of God in all the world, and the successful conclusion of our beloved Guardian's world-encircling Crusade, enabling his lovers and loved ones everywhere to lay this glorious harvest of victory in his name at the feet of the Blessed Beauty. This Most Great Jubilee is the crowning victory of the life work of Shoghi Effendi, Guardian of the Cause of God. He it was, and he alone, who unfolded the potentialities of the widely scattered, numerically small, and largely unorganized Bahá'í community which had been called into being during the Heroic Age of the Faith. He it was who unfolded the grand design of God's Holy Cause; set in motion the great plans of teaching already outlined by 'Abdu'l-Bahá; established the institutions and greatly extended the endowments at the World Center, and raised the Temples of America, Africa, Australasia, and Europe; developed the Administrative Order of the Cause throughout the world; and set the ark of the Cause true on its course. He appointed the Hands of the Cause of God.

The paeans of joy and gratitude, of love and adoration which we now raise to the throne of Bahá'u'lláh would be inadequate, and the celebrations of this Most Great Jubilee in which, as promised by our beloved Guardian, we are now engaged would be marred, were no tribute paid at this time to the Hands of the Cause of God. For they share the victory with their beloved commander, he who raised them up and appointed them. They kept the ship on its course and brought it safe to port. The Universal House of Justice, with pride and love, recalls on this supreme occasion its profound admiration for the heroic work which they have accomplished. We do not wish to dwell on the appalling dangers which faced the infant Cause when it was suddenly deprived of our beloved Shoghi Effendi, but rather to acknowledge with all the love and gratitude of our hearts the reality of the sacrifice, the labor, the self-discipline, the superb stewardship of the Hands of the Cause of God. We can think of no more fitting words to express our tribute to these dearly loved and valiant souls than to recall the words of Bahá'u'lláh Himself: "Light and glory, greeting and praise be upon the Hands of His Cause, through whom the light of long-suffering hath shone forth, and the declaration of authority is proven of God, the powerful, the mighty, the independent; and through whom the sea of bestowal hath moved, and the breeze of the favor of God, the Lord of mankind, hath wafted."

The members of the Universal House of Justice, all being in Haifa at the time of the election, were able to visit the Holy Shrines of Bahá'u'lláh, the Báb, and of 'Abdu'l-Bahá, where they prostrated themselves at the Sacred Thresholds and humbly sought strength and assistance in the mighty task before them. Later, in London, they have paid homage at the resting-place of Shoghi Effendi, the blessed and sacred bough of the Tree of Holiness.

As soon as the House of Justice is able to organize its work and deploy its forces, it will examine carefully all the conditions of the Cause of God, and communications will be made to the friends. At this time we call upon the believers everywhere to follow up vigorously the opportunities opened up by the World Crusade. Consolidation and deepening must go hand in hand with an eager extension of the teaching work so that the onward march of the Cause may continue unabated in preparation for future plans. Now that the attention of the public is becoming more and more drawn to the Cause of God, the friends must brace themselves and prepare their institutions to sustain the gaze of the world, whether it be friendly or hostile, eager or idle.

The Universal House of Justice greets you all lovingly and joyfully at this time, and asks you to pray fervently for its speedy development and the spiritual strengthening of its members.

Message to National Conventions—1963

The marvelous happenings which have transpired during and immediately after the twelve days of Riḍván attest the greatness of the Cause of God, and fill every Baháʼí heart to overflowing with joy and gratitude. It was in obedience to the summons of the Lord of Hosts Himself that the elected representatives of the fifty-six national and regional communities of the Baháʼí world were called to elect, in the shadow of God's Holy Mountain and in the house of the Center of His Covenant, the members of the Universal House of Justice. It was the Sign of God on earth, the Dayspring of Divine Guidance, the Guardian of the Cause of God, who gathered more than six thousand Baháʼís from all parts of the earth to the celebration of the Most Great Jubilee in London.

The first of these historic occasions was marked by events of extreme spiritual and administrative significance at the World Center of the Faith. The daily visits of large groups of believers, of many varying backgrounds, to the sacred shrines in the twin holy cities; the holding of the first International Baháʼí Convention and the successful accomplishment of its main task; the celebration of the Riḍván Feast by some three hundred believers in the company of the Hands of the Cause of God in the precincts of the Ḥaram-i-Aqdas, are events of unique character and untold significance in the history of our beloved Faith.

The celebration of the Most Great Jubilee in London must be described elsewhere. Suffice it to say now that this greatest gathering of Baháʼís ever held in one place was permeated by a spirit of such bliss as could only have come from the outpourings of the Abhá Kingdom. The review of the progress of the Cause; the presentation of believers from the new races and countries of the world brought within the pale of the Faith during the beloved Guardian's Ten Year Crusade, of the Knights of Bahá'u'lláh, those valiant souls who carried the banner of Bahá'u'lláh to the unopened and often inhospitable regions of the earth; the spontaneous outbursts of singing of "Alláh-u-Abhá," the informal gatherings, the constant greetings of Bahá'u'lláh's warriors known to each other only by name and service; the youth gatherings; the unprecedented publicity in the press, on radio and television; the daily stream of visitors to the beloved Guardian's resting-place; the radiant faces and heightened awareness of the true and real brotherhood of the human race within the Kingdom of the Everlasting Father, are among the outstanding events of this supreme occasion, the crowning victory of the life work of Shoghi Effendi.

REAFFIRMING A TRIBUTE

The Universal House of Justice wishes to reaffirm at this time the tribute which it felt moved to pay to the Hands of the Cause of God at the World Congress, those precious souls who have brought the Cause safely to victory in the name of Shoghi Effendi. We wish also to remember the devoted work of their Auxiliary Board members, as well as the services of the Knights of Bahá'u'lláh, of the army of pioneers, the members of the national and regional spiritual assemblies, the services and prayers and sacrifices of the believers everywhere, all of which in the sum total have attracted such bounties and favors from Bahá'u'lláh.

The Universal House of Justice, in several sessions held in the Holy Land and in London, has been able to initiate its work and to make arrangements for the establishment of the institution in Haifa. It has no officers and henceforth its communications to the Bahá'í world will be signed UNIVERSAL HOUSE OF JUSTICE over an embossed seal.

The Cause of God, launched on the sea of the Divine Plan of 'Abdu'l-Bahá, has achieved, under the superb leadership of its beloved Guardian, a spread throughout the world and a momentum which must now carry it forward on the next stage of its world-redeeming mission, the second epoch of the Divine Plan. The Universal House of Justice, in close consultation with the Hands of the Cause, is examining the vast range of Bahá'í activity and growth in order to prepare a detailed plan of expansion for the whole Bahá'í community, to be launched at Riḍván 1964. But there are some objectives to be achieved at once.

IMMEDIATE OBJECTIVES

The consolidation of the goals and new communities of the Bahá'í world is an urgent and immediate task facing the fifty-six national spiritual assemblies, and an essential preparation for the launching of the new plans. Pioneers must be maintained at their posts and all the local spiritual assemblies strengthened through a firm establishment of Bahá'í community life and an active teaching program. Those national spiritual assemblies which rest on the basis of a small number of local spiritual assemblies must make great efforts to insure that this number will be increased at Riḍván 1964. Pioneers ready to go to consolidation areas, as well as those eager to open new territories, should make their offers through their national spiritual assembly.

The great work of teaching must be extended, not only in those areas where mass conversion is beginning, but everywhere. The high intensity of teaching activity reached at the end of the World Crusade, far from slackening, must now be increased as the friends everywhere draw on the vast spiritual powers released as a result of the celebration of the Most Great Jubilee and the emergence of the Universal House of Justice.

The Ten Year Crusade witnessed the completion of the structure of the Mother Temple of Europe. It is now imperative to complete, without delay, the interior decoration, to install utilities and lay access roads, to landscape grounds, and to construct the caretaker's house. This work will cost not less than $210,000, but if delayed it will cost considerably more. The House of Justice calls upon the national spiritual assemblies to allocate substantial budgets for the immediate completion of this work.

PROJECTS TO BE EMBARKED UPON

The plan to be embarked upon next Riḍván, the details of which will be announced during the coming year, will include such projects as the extension and embellishment of the endowments at the World Center; collation of the writings of Bahá'u'lláh, 'Abdu'l-Bahá, and Shoghi Effendi; continual reinforcement of the ties binding the Bahá'í world to the United Nations; formation of many more national spiritual assemblies, both by division of existing regional spiritual assemblies and the development of new Bahá'í communities, together with the purchase of national Ḥaẓíratu'l-Quds, Temple sites, and national endowments; the opening of new territories to the Faith; detailed plans for national spiritual assemblies involving, in some areas, consolidation goals, in others the multiplication of Bahá'í institutes and schools, in others a great enrichment of Bahá'í literature, and in all a vast increase in the number of Bahá'ís, and the holding of oceanic and intercontinental conferences.

All such expansion and development of the Faith will

be dependent upon the Bahá'í Fund. The Universal House of Justice calls the attention of every believer to this vital and pressing matter, and asks the national spiritual assemblies to pay special attention to the principle of universal participation, so that every single follower of Bahá'u'lláh may make his offering, however small or great, and thereby identify himself with the work of the Cause everywhere. It is our hope that a constant flow of contributions to the International Fund will make it possible to build up sufficient reserves for the launching of the new plan in 1964.

Beloved friends, we enter the second epoch of the Divine Plan blessed beyond compare, riding the crest of a great wave of victory produced for us by our beloved Guardian. The Cause of God is now firmly rooted in the world. Forward then, confident in the power and protection of the Lord of Hosts, Who will, through storm and trial, toil and jubilee, use His devoted followers to bring to a despairing humanity the life-giving waters of His supreme Revelation.

[May 7, 1963—(London)]

Seat of the Universal House of Justice; New Arrangements for Pilgrims

The Universal House of Justice has been deeply moved and its hopes have been raised high by the many messages of love, devotion, and eager anticipation which have been received from national conventions and national spiritual assemblies.

Two decisions have been taken by the Universal House of Justice involving a further development of the institutions at the World Center. The former offices of the International Bahá'í Council at 10 Haparsim Street being inadequate for the far greater volume of work facing the Universal House of Justice, it has been decided to take over the whole of this building (until now called the Western Pilgrim House) as the seat, for the present time, of the Universal House of Justice.

This decision made it necessary to find other accommodation for the western pilgrims and led directly to the second decision. After careful consideration of the alternatives, the House of Justice has decided that the time has come to take the significant step, anticipated by our beloved Guardian, of housing all pilgrims in one place. It was found possible, by slight alterations, to accommodate all pilgrims, without lessening the number, in the former Eastern Pilgrim House and its adjacent buildings. We have therefore established one Pilgrim House, at the Bahá'í gardens on Mount Carmel. The friends should note that this is where they should go on arrival.

All friends whose pilgrimages have been confirmed for

1963-64 are therefore expected. There are still vacancies after December 1963, but only a very few before that date.

We have asked the Hands of the Cause residing in the Holy Land to continue to be responsible for the program of the pilgrims while they are here, but letters requesting permission to come should be addressed to the Universal House of Justice.

[June 16, 1963*]

[*In April 1969 a new action was taken by the Universal House of Justice to open the door of pilgrimage to a greater number of believers, and instructions were given the national spiritual assemblies concerning procedures to be followed.*]

The Guardianship

We wish to share with you the text of the following resolution:

"After prayerful and careful study of the Holy Texts bearing upon the question of the appointment of the successor to Shoghi Effendi as Guardian of the Cause of God, and after prolonged consultation which included consideration of the views of the Hands of the Cause of God residing in the Holy Land, the Universal House of Justice finds that there is no way to appoint or to legislate to make it possible to appoint a second Guardian to succeed Shoghi Effendi."

Please share this message with the friends in your jurisdiction.

[October 6, 1963]*

Second World-Encircling Enterprise

Six years ago when nearing the midway point of the Ten Year Crusade, the Bahá'í world found itself abruptly deprived of the guiding hand of its beloved Guardian. The anguish which then seized our hearts, far from paralyzing the progress of the Cause, stiffened our resolve and fired our zeal to complete the tasks which God, through His Chosen Branch, had laid upon us. The august institution of the Hands of the Cause of God, which he had, but recently, in compliance with the instruction of the Master's Will, raised up, kept the people of this Cause faithfully to the path which had been shown to us by the pen of Divine guidance, and brought us not only to the triumphal conclusion of that Crusade but to the culminating point of the construction of the framework of Bahá'u'lláh's World Order.

In March 1930 Shoghi Effendi wrote that Bahá'u'lláh and 'Abdu'l-Bahá had "in unequivocal and emphatic language, appointed those twin institutions of the House of Justice and of the Guardianship as Their chosen successors, destined to apply the principles, promulgate the laws, protect the institutions, adapt loyally and intelligently the Faith to the requirements of progressive society, and consummate the incorruptible inheritance which the Founders of the Faith have bequeathed to the world." After long and prayerful consultation, the House of Justice, as the friends have already been informed, found that there is no way in which it can legislate for a second Guardian to succeed Shoghi Effendi. The Universal House of Justice has therefore begun, in humble obedience to the will of God, and strengthened by daily prayer in the holy shrines, to undertake the heavy tasks laid upon it. In the words of our beloved Guardian it "will guide, organize, and unify the affairs of the Movement throughout the world" and "will have to consider afresh the whole situation, and lay down the principle which shall direct, so long as it deems advisable, the affairs of the Cause."

Covenant of Bahá'u'lláh

The Covenant of Bahá'u'lláh is unbroken, its all-encompassing power inviolate. The two unique features which distinguish it from all religious covenants of the past are unchanged and operative. The revealed Word, in its original purity, amplified by the divinely guided interpretations of 'Abdu'l-Bahá and Shoghi Effendi, remains immutable, unadulterated by any man-made creeds or dogmas, unwarrantable inferences, or unauthorized interpretations. The channel of Divine guidance, providing flexibility in all the affairs of mankind, remains open through that institution which was founded by Bahá'u'lláh and endowed by Him with supreme authority and unfailing guidance, and of which the Master wrote: "Unto this body all things must be referred." How clearly we can see the truth of Bahá'u'lláh's assertion: "The Hand of Omnipotence hath established His Revelation upon an enduring foundation. Storms of human strife are powerless to undermine its basis, nor will men's fanciful theories succeed in damaging its structure."

Responsibility of the Institutions

As the significance of the Cause of God continues in the years ahead to become more clearly apparent to the eyes of men, a great responsibility to watch over its security rests upon all of its institutions. The institution of the Hands of the Cause of God, charged in the Sacred Texts with the specific duties of protecting and propagating the Faith, has a particularly vital responsibility to discharge. In their capacity as protectors of the Faith, the Hands will continue to take action to expel Covenant-breakers and to reinstate those who sincerely repent, subject in each instance to the approval of the Universal House of Justice. Exercising their function of propagating the Faith, the Hands of the Cause will inspire, advise, and assist the national spiritual assemblies in the work as they did in the time of our beloved Shoghi Effendi, assisted by the members of their Auxiliary Boards, who will continue to fulfill those functions outlined for them by him.

We stand now upon the threshold of the second epoch of 'Abdu'l-Bahá's Divine Plan, with the outposts of the Cause established in the remotest corners of the earth, and having already witnessed the beginnings of that entry into the Faith by troops promised by the Master Himself. The foundation of the Kingdom has been securely laid, the framework has been raised. The friends must now consolidate these achievements, safeguard their institutions, and gather the peoples and kindreds of the world into the ark which the Hand of God has built.

SECOND WORLD-ENCIRCLING ENTERPRISE

Next Riḍván will be launched the second of those world-encircling enterprises destined in the course of time to carry the Word of God to every human soul. The standard bearers of this Nine Year Plan are the Hands of the Cause of God. The responsibility for directing the work will rest upon the shoulders of the national spiritual assemblies, the generals of the army of Light, under the guidance of the Universal House of Justice.

As the first step inaugurating this great undertaking we

rejoice to announce the formation next Riḍván of nineteen national spiritual assemblies, resulting in the dissolution of six of the existing regional national spiritual assemblies, and bringing the total number of these pillars of the Universal House of Justice to sixty-nine. The national and regional national assemblies now to be formed are:

1. The National Spiritual Assembly of the Bahá'ís of North West Africa, with its seat in Tunis, comprising Tunisia, Algeria, Morocco, Spanish Sahara, Rio de Oro, Mauritania, the Canary Is., and Madeira.
2. The National Spiritual Assembly of the Bahá'ís of West Africa, with its seat in Monrovia, comprising Liberia, Sénégal, Gambia, Portuguese Guinea, Guinea, Sierra Leone, Mali, Upper Volta, Ivory Coast, and Cape Verde Is.
3. The National Spiritual Assembly of the Bahá'ís of West Central Africa, with its seat in Victoria, comprising Cameroon, Spanish Guinea, St. Thomas I., Fernando Po I., Corisco I., Nigeria, Niger, Dahomey, Togo, and Ghana.
4. The National Spiritual Assembly of the Bahá'ís of Uganda and Central Africa, with its seat in Kampala, comprising Uganda, Rwanda, Burundi, the Republic of the Congo (Ex-Belgian), the Congo Republic (Ex-French), Central African Republic, Gabon, and Chad.
5. The National Spiritual Assembly of the Bahá'ís of Kenya, with its seat in Nairobi.
6. The National Spiritual Assembly of the Bahá'ís of Tanganyika and Zanzibar, with its seat in Dar-es-Salaam, comprising Tanganyika, Zanzibar, Mafia I., and Pemba I.

7. The National Spiritual Assembly of the Bahá'ís of South Central Africa, with its seat in Salisbury, comprising Nyasaland, Northern Rhodesia, Southern Rhodesia, and Bechuanaland.
8. The National Spiritual Assembly of the Bahá'ís of South and West Africa, with its seat in Johannesburg, comprising Angola, South West Africa, South Africa, Zululand, Swaziland, Basutoland, Mozambique, and St. Helena.
9. The National Spiritual Assembly of the Bahá'ís of the Indian Ocean, with its seat in Port Louis, comprising Mauritius, the Malagasy Republic, Réunion I., Seychelles Is., Comoro Is., and the Chagos Archipelago.
10. The National Spiritual Assembly of the Bahá'ís of the Hawaiian Islands, with its seat in Honolulu.
11. The National Spiritual Assembly of the Bahá'ís of the South Pacific Ocean, with its seat in Suva, comprising the Gilbert and Ellice Is., Nauru I., Fiji, Samoa Is., Tonga Is., and Cook Is.
12. The National Spiritual Assembly of the Bahá'ís of the South West Pacific Ocean, with its seat in Honiara, comprising the Solomon Is., New Hebrides Is., New Caledonia, and Loyalty Is.
13. The National Spiritual Assembly of the Bahá'ís of North East Asia, with its seat in Tokyo, comprising Japan, Formosa, Hong Kong, and Macau.
14. The National Spiritual Assembly of the Bahá'ís of Korea, with its seat in Seoul.
15. The National Spiritual Assembly of the Bahá'ís of Malaysia, with its seat in Kuala Lumpur, comprising Malaya, Singapore, Brunei, Sabah, and Sarawak.
16. The National Spiritual Assembly of the Bahá'ís of

Second World-Encircling Enterprise 17

Indonesia, with its seat in Djakarta, comprising Indonesia, the Mentawai Is., Portuguese Timor, and West Irian.
17. The National Spiritual Assembly of the Bahá'ís of Viet Nam, with its seat in Saigon, and having jurisdiction over the Bahá'ís of Cambodia.
18. The National Spiritual Assembly of the Bahá'ís of Thailand, with its seat in Bangkok, and having jurisdiction over the Bahá'ís of Laos.
19. The National Spiritual Assembly of the Bahá'ís of the Philippines, with its seat in Manila.

The detailed goals of the Plan, which will include sixty-nine national plans, have yet to be announced, but they must be such as to develop still further the World Center of the Faith and the work of its institutions; to consolidate those territories which have already been opened to the Faith; to bring God's healing Message to many more of the peoples and territories of the world including all the unopened territories of the Ten Year Crusade and all the remaining independent states of the planet; and to achieve worldwide proclamation of the Faith to mark the Centenary of Bahá'u'lláh's Proclamation to the kings and rulers in 1867-1868.

In the spring of 1968 the next election for the Universal House of Justice will take place.

THIRD EPOCH OF FORMATIVE AGE

Beloved friends, the Cause of God, guarded and nurtured since its inception by God's Messengers, by the Center of His Covenant, and by His Sign on earth, now enters a new epoch, the third of the Formative Age. It must now grow rapidly in size, increase its spiritual cohesion and executive ability, develop its institutions, and extend its influence into all strata of society. We, its members, must, by constant study of the life-giving Word, and by dedicated service, deepen in spiritual understanding and show to the world a mature, responsible, fundamentally assured, and happy way of life, far removed from the passions, prejudices, and distractions of present-day society. Relying upon God alone, we can promote His Cause and establish His Kingdom on earth. Only thus can we prove our love for Those Who brought this new Day into being. Only thus can we prove the truth of Their Divine Mission and demonstrate how valid was Their sacrifice.

[October 1963]

A Service Every Believer Can Render

With the rapid approach of the launching of the Nine Year Plan, the Universal House of Justice feels that it is timely to lay clearly before the Bahá'ís of all countries the needs of the Fund at all its levels: local, national, continental, and international.

The continual expansion of the Faith and the diversification of the activities of Bahá'í communities make it more and more necessary for every believer to ponder carefully his responsibilities and contribute as much and as regularly as he or she can. Contributing to the Fund is a service that every believer can render, be he poor or wealthy; for this is a spiritual responsibility in which the amount given is not important. It is the degree of the sacrifice of the giver, the love with which he makes his gift, and the unity of all the friends in this service which bring spiritual confirmations. As the beloved Guardian wrote in August 1957: "All, no matter how modest their resources, must participate. Upon the degree of self-sacrifice involved in these individual contributions will directly depend the efficacy and the spiritual influence which these nascent administrative institutions, called into being through the power of Bahá'u'lláh, and by virtue of the design conceived by the Center of His Covenant, will exert."

Not only the individual's responsibility to contribute is important at this time, but also the uses to which the fund is put and the areas in which it is expended.

Much of the present rapid expansion of the Faith is taking place in areas of great poverty where the believers, however much they sacrifice, cannot produce sufficient funds to sustain the work. It is these very areas which are the most fruitful in teaching, and a sum of money spent here will produce ten times—even a hundred times—the results obtainable in other parts of the world. Yet in the past months the Universal House of Justice has had to refuse a number of appeals for assistance from such areas because there just was not enough money in the International Fund.

It should therefore be the aim of every local and national community to become not only self-supporting, but to expend its funds with such wisdom and economy as to be able to contribute substantially to the Bahá'í International Fund, thus enabling the House of Justice to aid the work in fruitful but impoverished areas, to assist new national assemblies to start their work, to contribute to major international undertakings of the Nine Year Plan such as oceanic conferences, and to carry forward the work of beautifying the land surrounding the holy shrines at the World Center of the Faith.

Nor should the believers, individually or in their assemblies, forget the vitally important continental funds which provide for the work of the Hands of the Cause of God and their Auxiliary Boards. This divine institution, so assiduously fostered by the Guardian, and which has already played a unique role in the history of the Faith, is destined to render increasingly important services in the years to come.

In the midst of a civilization torn by strifes and enfeebled by materialism, the people of Bahá are building a new world. We face at this time opportunities and responsibilities of vast magnitude and great urgency. Let each believer in his inmost heart resolve not to be seduced by the ephemeral allurements of the society around him, nor to

A Service Every Believer Can Render 21

be drawn into its feuds and short-lived enthusiasms, but instead to transfer all he can from the old world to that new one which is the vision of his longing and will be the fruit of his labors.

[December 18, 1963]

Call to Action—Nine Year Plan

The divinely propelled process, described in such awe-inspiring words by our beloved Guardian, which began six thousand years ago at the dawn of the Adamic Cycle and which is destined to culminate in "the stage at which the light of God's triumphant Faith shining in all its power and glory will have suffused and enveloped the entire planet," is now entering its tenth and last part.

The Ten Year Crusade, so recently consummated in a blaze of victory and rejoicing, constituted the entire ninth part of this process. It saw the Cause of God leap forward in one mighty decade-long effort to the point at which the foundations of its Administrative Order were laid throughout the world, thus preparing the way for that awakening of the masses which must characterize the future progress of the Faith.

From the beginning of this Dispensation the most urgent summons of the Word of God, voiced successively by the Báb and Bahá'u'lláh, has been to teach the Cause. 'Abdu'l-Bahá, in His own words, "spent His days and nights in promoting the Cause and urging the peoples to service." Shoghi Effendi, discharging the sacred mission laid upon him, raised the Administrative Order of the Faith, already enshrined within the Sacred Writings, and forged it into a teaching instrument to accomplish through a succession of plans, national, international, and global, the entire Divine Plan of 'Abdu'l-Bahá, and he clearly foresaw in the "tremendously long" tenth part of the process already referred to a series of plans to be launched by the Universal

Call to Action—Nine Year Plan 23

House of Justice, extending over "successive epochs of both the Formative and Golden Ages of the Faith."

The first of these plans is now before us. Opening at Riḍván 1964, while the memories of the glorious Jubilee of 1963 still surge within our hearts, it must, during its nine-year course, witness a huge expansion of the Cause of God and universal participation by all believers in the life of that Cause.

Tasks at the World Center

At the World Center of the Faith the tasks of the Plan include:

> Publication of a synopsis and codification of the Kitáb-i-Aqdas, the Most Holy Book;
>
> Formulation of the constitution of the Universal House of Justice;
>
> Development of the institution of the Hands of the Cause of God, in consultation with the body of the Hands of the Cause, with a view to the extension into the future of its appointed functions of protection and propagation;
>
> Continued collation and classification of the Bahá'í Sacred Scriptures as well as of the writings of Shoghi Effendi;
>
> Continued efforts directed towards the emancipation of the Faith from the fetters of religious orthodoxy and its recognition as an independent religion;
>
> The preparation of a plan for the befitting development and beautification of the entire area of Bahá'í property surrounding the holy shrines;

Extension of the existing gardens on Mount Carmel;

Development of the relationship between the Bahá'í Community and the United Nations;

The holding of oceanic and intercontinental conferences;

The coordination of worldwide plans to commemorate, in 1967/68, the centenary of Bahá'u'lláh's Proclamation to the kings and rulers which centered round His revelation of the Súriy-i-Mulúk in Adrianople.

TASKS FOR THE WORLD COMMUNITY

In the world community the Plan involves:

The opening of seventy virgin territories and the resettlement of twenty-four;

The raising of the number of national spiritual assemblies, the pillars sustaining the Universal House of Justice, to one hundred and eight, nine times the number which embarked on the first historic World Crusade in 1953;

Increasing the number of local spiritual assemblies to over thirteen thousand seven hundred, scattered throughout the territories and islands of the world, at least one thousand seven hundred of them to be incorporated;

The raising of the number of localities where Bahá'ís reside to over fifty-four thousand;

The building of two more Mashriqu'l-Adhkárs, one in Asia and one in Latin America;

The acquisition of:
    Thirty-two teaching institutes,

Call to Action—Nine Year Plan

Fifty-two national Ḥaẓíratu'l-Quds,
Fifty-four national endowments, and
Sites for sixty-two future Temples;

Wide extension of recognition by civil authorities of the Bahá'í holy days and Bahá'í marriage certificates;

The translation of literature into one hundred and thirty-three more languages, and its enrichment in major languages into which translations have already been made;

The establishment of four new Bahá'í publishing trusts, and

A vast increase in the financial resources of the Faith.

The Role of the Individual

The healthy development of the Cause requires that this great expansion be accompanied by the dedicated effort of every believer in teaching, in living the Bahá'í life, in contributing to the Fund, and particularly in the persistent effort to understand more and more the significance of Bahá'u'lláh's Revelation. In the words of our beloved Guardian, "One thing and only one thing will unfailingly and alone secure the undoubted triumph of this sacred Cause, namely, the extent to which our own inner life and private character mirror forth in their manifold aspects the splendor of those eternal principles proclaimed by Bahá'u'lláh."

Twin Objectives of the Nine Year Plan

Expansion and universal participation are the twin objectives of this initial phase of the second epoch of the Divine Plan, and all the goals assigned to the sixty-nine national communities are contributory to them. The process of cooperation between national spiritual assemblies, already intitiated by the beloved Guardian, will, during the course of this Plan, apply to over two hundred specific projects and will further strengthen this process which may well assume great importance in future stages of the Formative Age.

Once more, dear friends, we enter the battle, but with an incomparably greater array than that which embarked upon the World Crusade in 1953. To that small force of twelve national communities, now veteran campaigners, have been added fifty-seven new legions, each under the generalship of a national spiritual assembly, each destined to become a veteran of this and future campaigns. That Crusade began with slightly more than six hundred local spiritual assemblies, the greater part of which were situated in Persia, North America, and Europe; the home fronts now comprise nearly four thousand six hundred local spiritual assemblies scattered throughout the continents and islands of the world. We begin this Plan with a tremendous momentum, exemplified by the addition, since last Riḍván, of over four thousand new centers and thirteen national spiritual assemblies, and by the beginning, in several countries, of that entry by troops into the Cause of God prophesied by 'Abdu'l-Bahá and so eagerly anticipated by Him.

The standard bearers of this Nine Year Plan are those same divinely appointed, tried, and victorious souls who bore the standard of the World Crusade, the Hands of the Cause of God, whose advice and consultation have been invaluable in the working out of this Nine Year Plan. Supported by their "deputies, assistants, and advisers," the members of the Auxiliary Boards, they will inspire and protect the army of God, lead through every breach to the limit of available resources, and sustain those communities struggling over intractable or stony ground, so that by 1973 the celebrations befitting the centenary of the revelation of the Most Holy Book may be undertaken by a victorious, firmly established, organically united world community, dedicated to the service of God and the final triumph of His Cause.

Therefore let each of the sixty-nine communities seize its tasks, at once consider how best to accomplish them within the allotted span, raise its band of pioneers, consecrate itself to unremitting labor, and set out on its mission. Now is the golden opportunity. For whatever convulsions the waywardness of a godless and materialistic age may yet precipitate in the world, however grievous may be the effects of the rolling up of the present order on the plans and efforts of the community of the Most Great Name, we must seize the opportunities of the hour and go forward confident that all things are within His mighty grasp and that, if we but play our part, total and unconditional victory will inevitably be ours.

[Riḍván 1964]

Dedication of the Mother Temple of Europe

We have just witnessed the dedication of the Mother Temple of Europe—a project of untold significance and tremendous potential for the spread of the light of God's Faith in that continent. One of the major achievements called for by our beloved Guardian at the outset of the Ten Year Crusade, this Mas̲h̲riqu'l-Ad̲h̲kár was triumphantly raised during its closing years as the fruit of long and arduous labors in the face of determined opposition and upon the sacrificial gifts of believers from all parts of the world. Now dedicated in the opening months of the Nine Year Plan, it forms a striking link between these two great crusades, demonstrating afresh the organic progress of the Cause whereby the efforts exerted in one period bear fruit in the next, which in turn endow the Bahá'í community with new and greater capacities for the winning of still greater victories.

You are now gathered in this conference to deliberate on ways and means of accomplishing the goals which are set before you. Let every believer, as he considers in detail these various goals, bear in mind four supreme objectives: to carry the Message of Bahá'u'lláh to every stratum of society, not only in the towns and cities but also in the villages and country districts where the virus of materialism has had much less effect on the lives of men; to take urgent, wise, and well-considered steps to spread the Faith to those countries of Eastern Europe in which it has not yet become established; to reinforce strongly the heroic band of pioneers in the islands of the Mediterranean and the North Sea—islands which are to play such an important role in the awakening of the entire continent—as well as to prosecute energetically the goals you are called upon to achieve in other continents and oceans; and to foster the cooperation between national communities and between national spiritual assemblies and the Hands of the Cause of God which has contributed so markedly to the work of the Faith on that continent and is so essential for its future development.

Above all, let every European Bahá'í have ever-present in his mind that these are the five years during which Bahá'u'lláh sojourned on the soil of that continent a century ago. Let him resolve so to deepen his knowledge of the Faith and so to increase his standards of self-sacrifice and dedication to the Cause as to play his part in building a community which will be worthy of this supreme bounty and which will be a beacon light to the peoples of this fear-wracked world.

In 1953 Shoghi Effendi wrote that the continent of Europe had "at last at this critical hour—this great turning point in its fortunes—entered upon what may well be regarded as the opening phase of a great spiritual revival that bids fair to eclipse any period in its spiritual history." Those who have been privileged to witness the extraordinary strengthening and consolidation of the Cause in Europe during the course of the last eleven years are well aware of the reservoir of spiritual potential that has been building up and the transformation of the life of the European Bahá'í community that has ensued. May the completion and dedication of the Mashriqu'l-Adhkár be the signal for the unleashing of this potential, bringing about on the European mainland and in the islands around its shores a quickening of the process of individual conversion comparable to those events which have transpired with such astonishing suddenness in other continents of the globe.

[July 1964]

[*The above message was addressed to those gathered in the European Teaching Conference called on the occasion of the dedication of the Mother Temple of Europe.*]

Teaching the Masses

When the masses of mankind are awakened and enter the Faith of God, a new process is set in motion and the growth of a new civilization begins. Witness the emergence of Christianity and of Islám. These masses are the rank and file, steeped in traditions of their own, but receptive to the new Word of God, by which, when they truly respond to it, they become so influenced as to transform those who come in contact with them.

God's standards are different from those of men. According to men's standards, the acceptance of any cause by people of distinction, of recognized fame and status, determines the value and greatness of that cause. But, in the words of Bahá'u'lláh: "The summons and Message which We gave were never intended to reach or to benefit one land or one people only. Mankind in its entirety must firmly adhere to whatsoever has been revealed and vouchsafed unto it." Or again, "He has endowed every soul with the capacity to recognize the signs of God. How could He, otherwise, have fulfilled His testimony unto men, if ye be of them that ponder His Cause in their hearts." In countries where teaching the masses has succeeded, the Bahá'ís have poured out their time and effort in village areas to the same extent as they had formerly done in cities and towns. The results indicate how unwise it is to solely concentrate on one section of the population. Each national assembly therefore should so balance its resources and harmonize its efforts that the Faith of God is taught not only to those who are readily accessible but to all sections of society, however remote they may be.

The unsophisticated people of the world—and they form the large majority of its population—have the same right to know of the Cause of God as others. When the friends are teaching the Word of God they should be careful to give the Message in the same simplicity as it is enunciated in our teachings. In their contacts they must show genuine and divine love. The heart of an unlettered soul is extremely sensitive; any trace of prejudice on the part of the pioneer or teacher is immediately sensed.

When teaching among the masses, the friends should be careful not to emphasize the charitable and humanitarian aspects of the Faith as a means to win recruits. Experience has shown that when facilities such as schools, dispensaries, hospitals, or even clothes and food are offered to the people being taught, many complications arise. The prime motive should always be the response of man to God's Message, and the recognition of His Messenger. Those who declare themselves as Bahá'ís should become enchanted with the beauty of the teachings, and touched by the love of Bahá'u'lláh. The declarants need not know all the proofs, history, laws, and principles of the Faith, but in the process of declaring themselves they must, in addition to catching the spark of faith, become basically informed about the Central Figures of the Faith, as well as the existence of laws they must follow and an administration they must obey.

After declaration, the new believers must not be left to their own devices. Through correspondence and dispatch of visitors, through conferences and training courses, these friends must be patiently strengthened and lovingly helped to develop into full Bahá'í maturity. The beloved Guardian, referring to the duties of Bahá'í assemblies in assisting the newly declared believer, has written: ". . . the members of each and every assembly should endeavor, by their patience, their love, their tact and wisdom, to nurse, subsequent to his admission, the newcomer into Bahá'í maturity, and win him over gradually to the unreserved acceptance of whatever has been ordained in the teachings."

Expansion and consolidation are twin processes that must go hand in hand. The friends must not stop expansion in the name of consolidation. Deepening the newly enrolled believers generates tremendous stimulus which results in further expansion. The enrollment of new believers, on the other hand, creates a new spirit in the community and provides additional potential manpower that will reinforce the consolidation work.

We would like to share with you some of the methods by national assemblies in various continents that have proved useful in teaching the masses, and attach a list. Certain of these may be valuable in your area, in addition to any methods you may yourself devise.

We are fervently praying that all national and local spiritual assemblies, supported by the individual believers, will achieve outstanding success in the fulfillment of this glorious objective.

[July 13, 1964]*

Teaching the Masses—Annex

1. Materials are sent at once to the new believers. In some places this material is in the form of printed cards, mainly in color, portraying a Bahá'í theme or principle. This helps the new believer to know that his declaration

has been accepted and to feel that he now belongs to the new Faith.

2. Training courses of about two weeks duration are held. To facilitate attendance and reduce cost, a number of villages are grouped together as one zone in which the course is held. The students to the courses are usually selected, so that the more capable participate and teaching is facilitated. Transportation expenses, feeding, and accommodation are provided if it is found that the participants are unable to cover such expenses themselves. The material to be taught is prepared ahead of time, presented in simple language, and translated into the vernacular. After the course, the more promising students are picked out and with their consent, are requested to undertake teaching projects for a limited period. It is sometimes found that long-term projects are also useful. These projects generally are carefully planned as to their duration, places to be visited, and material to be taught. If the traveling teachers are not able to cover their expenses, traveling and living expenses are provided by the Fund for the execution of a given and temporary teaching project.

3. Shorter training courses in the form of conferences over a long weekend are held.

4. These activities—training courses and conferences—are repeated as frequently as possible and are not dependent upon the acquisition of teaching institutes. In the absence of such institutes, these courses and conferences are normally held in Bahá'í homes or hired quarters, such as schools, etc. In order to facilitate the physical catering and accommodation of the participants, they are sometimes asked to come to the course with their eating utensils and bedding.

5. In the visits made to the villages, the visiting teacher meets with the local communities to give them basic Bahá'í

knowledge, such as living the Bahá'í life, the importance of teaching, prayer, fasting, Nineteen Day Feasts, Bahá'í elections, and contributions to the Fund. The question of contributions to the Fund is of utmost importance, so that the new believers may quickly feel themselves to be responsible members of the community. Each national assembly must find ways and means to stimulate the offering of contributions, in cash or kind, to make it easy for the friends to contribute and to give proper receipts to the donors.

These are but suggestions based on experience which may help you in your efforts to teach and deepen the spiritually starved multitudes in your area.

In the course of carrying out such a tremendous spiritual campaign among the masses, disappointments may well be encountered. We tabulate a few instances that have been brought to our notice:

a) Visiting pioneers or teachers may find, in some places, newly enrolled believers not so enthusiastic about their religion as expected, or not adjusting to standards of Bahá'í life, or they may find them thinking of material benefits they may hope to derive from their new membership. We should always remember that the process of nursing the believer into full spiritual maturity is slow, and needs loving education and patience.

b) Some teaching committees, in their eagerness to obtain results, place undue emphasis on obtaining a great number of declarations to the detriment of the quality of teaching.

c) Some traveling teachers, in their desire to show the result of their services, may not scrupulously teach their contacts, and in some rare cases, if, God forbid, they are insincere, may even give false reports.

Such irregularities have happened and can be repeated, but must not be a source of discouragement. By sending a team of teachers to an area, or by sending at intervals other teachers to those areas, and through correspondence and reports, such situations can be detected and immediately adjusted. The administration of the Faith must at all times keep in close touch with the teaching work.

To sum up:

1. Teaching the waiting masses is a reality facing each national assembly.

2. The friends must teach with conviction, determination, genuine love, lack of prejudice, and a simple language addressed to the heart.

3. Teaching must be followed up by training courses, conferences, and regular visits to deepen the believers in their knowledge of the teachings.

4. The close touch of the national office or teaching committees with the work is most essential, so that through reports and correspondence not only is information obtained and verified, but stimulation and encouragement is given.

5. Expansion and consolidation go hand in hand.

Universal Participation

In our message to you of April 1964, announcing the Nine Year Plan, we called attention to two major themes of that Plan, namely ". . . a huge expansion of the Cause of God and universal participation by all believers in the life of that Cause."

The enthusiastic vigor with which the believers throughout the world, under the devoted guidance of their national spiritual assemblies, have arisen to meet the challenge of the Plan, augurs well for the huge expansion called for. We now ask you to bend your efforts and thoughts, with equal enthusiasm, to the requirements of universal participation.

In that same message we indicated the meaning of universal participation: ". . . the dedicated effort of every believer in teaching, in living the Bahá'í life, in contributing to the Fund, and particularly in the persistent effort to understand more and more the significance of Bahá'u'lláh's Revelation. In the words of our beloved Guardian, 'One thing and only one thing will unfailingly and alone secure the undoubted triumph of this sacred Cause, namely, the extent to which our own inner life and private character mirror forth in their manifold aspects the splendor of those eternal principles proclaimed by Bahá'u'lláh.' "

"Regard the world as the human body," wrote Bahá'u'lláh to Queen Victoria. We can surely regard the Bahá'í world, the army of God, in the same way. In the human body, every cell, every organ, every nerve has its part to play. When all do so the body is healthy, vigorous, radiant, ready for every call made upon it. No cell, however humble, lives apart from the body, whether in serving it or receiving from it. This is true of the body of mankind in which God "has endowed each humble being with ability and talent," and is supremely true of the body of the Bahá'í world community, for this body is already an organism, united in its aspirations, unified in its methods, seeking assistance and confirmation from the same Source, and illumined with the conscious knowledge of its unity. Therefore, in this organic, divinely guided, blessed, and illumined body the participation of every believer is of the utmost importance, and is a source of power and vitality as yet unknown to us. For extensive and deep as has been the sharing in the glorious work of the Cause, who would claim that every single believer has succeeded in finding his or her fullest satisfaction in the life of the Cause? The Bahá'í world community, growing like a healthy new body, develops new cells, new organs, new functions and powers as it presses on to its maturity, when every soul, living for the Cause of God, will receive from that Cause, health, assurance, and the overflowing bounties of Bahá'u'lláh which are diffused through His divinely ordained Order.

In addition to teaching, every believer can pray. Every believer can strive to make his "own inner life and private character mirror forth in their manifold aspects the splendor of those eternal principles proclaimed by Bahá'u'lláh." Every believer can contribute to the Fund. Not all believers can give public talks, not all are called upon to serve on administrative institutions. But all can pray, fight their own spiritual battles, and contribute to the Fund. If every believer will carry out these sacred duties, we shall be astonished at the accession of power which will result to the whole body, and which in its turn will give rise to further growth and the showering of greater blessings on all of us.

The real secret of universal participation lies in the

Master's oft-expressed wish that the friends should love each other, constantly encourage each other, work together, be as one soul in one body, and in so doing become a true, organic, healthy body animated and illumined by the spirit. In such a body all will receive spiritual health and vitality from the organism itself, and the most perfect flowers and fruits will be brought forth.

Our prayers for the happiness and success of the friends everywhere are constantly offered at the holy shrines.

[September 1964]

Development of the Institution of the Hands of the Cause of God

Once again the World Center of our Faith has been the scene of historic events, affecting profoundly the immediate prosecution of the Nine Year Plan and the future development of the World Order of Bahá'u'lláh. The occasion was the gathering in the Holy Land, for a period of fourteen days, of the Hands of the Cause of God to discuss their vital responsibilities, and particularly as standard bearers of the Nine Year Plan.

The Universal House of Justice took advantage of this opportunity not only to receive the advice, opinions, and views of the Hands on the progress of the Nine Year Plan, but to consult them on the highly important goal announced by Riḍván 1964 under World Center goals as "Development of the institution of the Hands of the Cause of God, in consultation with the body of the Hands of the Cause, with a view to the extension into the future of its appointed functions of protection and propagation."

It was apparent that the elucidation of this vital goal, affecting as it does the relationship of the Hands of the Cause of God to all other institutions of the Cause, was imperative to the prosecution of the all-important teaching work and the development of the Bahá'í World Order.

Accordingly, the Universal House of Justice gave its full attention to this matter and, after study of the Sacred Texts and hearing the views of the Hands of the Cause themselves, has arrived at the following decisions:

Development of the Institution of the Hands

There is no way to appoint, or to legislate to make it possible to appoint, Hands of the Cause of God.

Responsibility for decisions of matters of general policy affecting the institution of the Hands of the Cause, which was formerly exercised by the beloved Guardian, now devolves upon the Universal House of Justice as the supreme and central institution of the Faith to which all must turn.

It is with great joy that we are able to share with you the initial steps now taken to attain the goal.

The assignment of the Hands to various continents remains unchanged, but, in order to expedite the work, the continents of Asia and the Western Hemisphere will each be divided into zones for the day-to-day work of the Hands, one or more Hands being responsible for each zone. Asia will consist of two zones: the Middle East, comprising the countries from and including Pakistan westwards and also Asiatic U.S.S.R.; and South and East Asia, comprising the remainder of the continent. The Western Hemisphere will consist of three zones: North America, Central America (including Mexico) and the Antilles, and South America. The Hawaiian friends will be included in the Australasian continental area, as listed in the recently issued statistical summary.

Members of Auxiliary Boards Increased

The number of members of the Auxiliary Boards for the propagation of the Faith will be increased in every continent, raising the total number of Auxiliary Board members in Africa from eighteen to twenty-seven; in Asia from fourteen to thirty-six; in Australasia from four to nine; in Europe from eighteen to twenty-seven; and in the Western Hemisphere from eighteen to thirty-six.

The Hands of the Cause in each continent are called upon to appoint one or more members of their Auxiliary Boards to act in an executive capacity on behalf of and in the name of each Hand, thereby assisting him in carrying out his work.

The exalted rank and specific functions of the Hands of the Cause of God make it inappropriate for them to be elected or appointed to administrative institutions, or to be elected as delegates to national conventions. Furthermore, it is their desire and the desire of the House of Justice that they be free to devote their entire energies to the vitally important duties conferred upon them in the Holy Writings. The importance of close collaboration between the Hands of the Cause and national spiritual assemblies cannot be overstressed, and a separate communication is being addressed to national assemblies on this subject, supplementing guidance given in earlier letters.

We anticipate announcing at Riḍván 1965 plans for oceanic and intercontinental conferences, an overall plan for worldwide proclamation of the Faith during 1967-68, the centenary year of the revelation of the Súriy-i-Mulúk, involving cooperation of national and local assemblies throughout the world, and conditions of entry for a competition for the design of the Mashriqu'l-Adhkár of Panama.

Teaching the masses is the greatest challenge now facing the followers of Bahá'u'lláh. No work is more important than that of carrying His Message with utmost speed to the bewildered and thirsting peoples of a spiritually parched world. Now, as the Hands return to their various continents, reinforced by a wider and more efficient organization of their work, we are confident that the whole Bahá'í world will, with rising enthusiasm and ever-increasing success, press forward with the teaching work, greatly increase the flow of pioneers, more widely participate in the financial support of the work of the Cause, and add rapidly to the list of goals already accomplished.

[November 1964]

Unassailable Foundation of the Cause of God

[*The following letter concerning questions about the Universal House of Justice was addressed to a National Spiritual Assembly and made available for the edification of the Bahá'ís throughout the world.*]

We are glad that you have brought to our attention the questions perplexing some of the believers. It is much better for these questions to be put freely and openly than to have them, unexpressed, burdening the hearts of devoted believers. Once one grasps certain basic principles of the Revelation of Bahá'u'lláh such uncertainties are easily dispelled. This is not to say that the Cause of God contains no mysteries. Mysteries there are indeed, but they are not of a kind to shake one's faith once the essential tenets of the Cause and the indisputable facts of any situation are clearly understood.

The questions put by the various believers fall into three groups. The first group centers upon the following queries: Why were steps taken to elect a Universal House of Justice with the foreknowledge that there would be no Guardian? Was the time ripe for such an action? Could not the International Bahá'í Council have carried on the work?

THE BASIS FOR ELECTION

At the time of our beloved Shoghi Effendi's death it was evident, from the circumstances and from the explicit requirements of the Holy Texts, that it had been impossible for him to appoint a successor in accordance with the provisions of the Will and Testament of 'Abdu'l-Bahá. This situation, in which the Guardian died without being able to appoint a successor, presented an obscure question not covered by the explicit Holy Text, and had to be referred to the Universal House of Justice. The friends should clearly understand that before the election of the Universal House of Justice there was no knowledge that there would be no Guardian. There could not have been any such foreknowledge, whatever opinions individual believers may have held. Neither the Hands of the Cause of God, nor the International Bahá'í Council, nor any other existing body could make a decision upon this all-important matter. Only the House of Justice had authority to pronounce upon it. This was one urgent reason for calling the election of the Universal House of Justice as soon as possible.

Following the passing of Shoghi Effendi the international administration of the Faith was carried on by the Hands of the Cause of God with the complete agreement and loyalty of the national spiritual assemblies and the body of the believers. This was in accordance with the Guardian's designation of the Hands as the "Chief Stewards of Bahá'u'lláh's embryonic World Commonwealth."

From the very outset of their custodianship of the Cause of God the Hands realized that since they had no certainty of Divine guidance such as is incontrovertibly assured to the Guardian and to the Universal House of Justice, their one safe course was to follow with undeviating firmness the instructions and policies of Shoghi Effendi. The entire history of religion shows no comparable record of such strict self-discipline, such absolute loyalty, and such complete self-abnegation by the leaders of a religion finding themselves suddenly deprived of their divinely inspired guide. The debt of gratitude which mankind for generations, nay, ages to come, owes to this handful of grief-stricken, steadfast, heroic souls is beyond estimation.

The Guardian had given the Bahá'í world explicit and detailed plans covering the period until Riḍván 1963, the end of the Ten Year Crusade. From that point onward, unless the Faith were to be endangered, further Divine guidance was essential. This was the second pressing reason for the calling of the election of the Universal House of Justice. The rightness of the time was further confirmed by references in Shoghi Effendi's letters to the Ten Year Crusade's being followed by other plans under the direction of the Universal House of Justice. One such reference is the following passage from a letter addressed to the National Spiritual Assembly of the British Isles on February 25, 1951, concerning its Two Year Plan which immediately preceded the Ten Year Crusade:

"On the success of this enterprise, unprecedented in its scope, unique in its character, and immense in its spiritual potentialities, must depend the initiation, at a later period in the Formative Age of the Faith, of undertakings embracing within their range all national assemblies functioning throughout the Bahá'í world, undertakings constituting in themselves a prelude to the launching of worldwide enterprises destined to be embarked upon, in future epochs of that same age, by the Universal House of Justice, that will symbolize the unity and coordinate and unify the activities of these national assemblies."

Having been in charge of the Cause of God for six years, the Hands, with absolute faith in the Holy Writings, called upon the believers to elect the Universal House of Justice, and even went so far as to ask that they themselves be not voted for. The sole, sad instance of anyone succumbing to the allurements of power was the pitiful attempt of Charles Mason Remey to usurp the Guardianship.

The following excerpts from a Tablet of 'Abdu'l-Bahá

Unassailable Foundation of the Cause of God

state clearly and emphatically the principles with which the friends are already familiar from the Will and Testament of the Master and the various letters of Shoghi Effendi, and explain the basis for the election of the Universal House of Justice. This Tablet was sent to Persia by the beloved Guardian himself, in the early years of his ministry, for circulation among the believers.

". . . for 'Abdu'l-Bahá is in a tempest of dangers and infinitely abhors differences of opinion . . . Praise be to God, there are no grounds for differences.

"The Báb, the Exalted One, is the Morn of Truth, the splendor of Whose light shineth through all regions. He is also the Harbinger of the Most Great Light, the Abhá Luminary. The Blessed Beauty is the One promised by the sacred books of the past, the revelation of the Source of light that shone upon Mount Sinai, Whose fire glowed in the midst of the Burning Bush. We are, one and all, servants of Their threshold, and stand each as a lowly keeper at Their door.

"My purpose is this, that ere the expiration of a thousand years, no one has the right to utter a single word, even to claim the station of Guardianship. The Most Holy Book is the Book to which all peoples shall refer, and in it the Laws of God have been revealed. Laws not mentioned in the Book should be referred to the decision of the Universal House of Justice. There will be no grounds for difference . . . Beware, beware lest anyone create a rift or stir up sedition. Should there be differences of opinion, the Supreme House of Justice would immediately resolve the problems. Whatever will be its decision, by majority vote, shall be the real truth, inasmuch as that House is under the protection, unerring guidance, and care of the one true Lord. He shall guard it from error and will protect it under the wing of His sanctity and infallibility. He who opposes it is cast out and will eventually be of the defeated.

"The Supreme House of Justice should be elected according to the system followed in the election of the parliaments of Europe. And when the countries would be guided the Houses of Justice of the various countries would elect the Supreme House of Justice.

"At whatever time all the beloved of God in each country appoint their delegates, and these in turn elect their representatives, and these representatives elect a body, that body shall be regarded as the Supreme House of Justice.

"The establishment of that House is not dependent upon the conversion of all the nations of the world. For example, if conditions were favorable and no disturbances would be caused, the friends in Persia would elect their representatives, and likewise the friends in America, in India, and other areas would also elect their representatives, and these would elect a House of Justice. That House of Justice would be the Supreme House of Justice. That is all." (Persian and Arabic Tablets of 'Abdu'l-Bahá, Vol. III, pp. 499-501)

The friends should realize that there is nothing in the Texts to indicate that the election of the Universal House of Justice could be called only by the Guardian. On the contrary, 'Abdu'l-Bahá envisaged the calling of its election in His own lifetime. At a time described by the Guardian as "the darkest moments of His (the Master's) life, under 'Abdu'l-Ḥamíd's regime, when He stood to be deported to the most inhospitable regions of Northern Africa," and when even His life was threatened, 'Abdu'l-Bahá wrote to Ḥájí Mírzá Taqí Afnán, the cousin of the Báb and chief builder of the 'Ishqábád Temple, commanding him to arrange for the election of the Universal House of Justice should the threats against the Master materialize. The second part of the Master's Will is also relevant to such a situation and should be studied by the friends.

THE INFALLIBILITY

The second series of problems vexing some of the friends centers on the question of the infallibility of the Universal House of Justice and its ability to function without the presence of the Guardian. Particular difficulty has been experienced in understanding the implications of the following statement by the beloved Guardian:

"Divorced from the institution of the Guardianship the World Order of Bahá'u'lláh would be mutilated and permanently deprived of that hereditary principle which, as 'Abdu'l-Bahá has written, has been invariably upheld by the Law of God. 'In all the Divine Dispensations,' He states, in a Tablet addressed to a follower of the Faith in Persia, 'the eldest son hath been given extraordinary distinctions. Even the station of prophethood hath been his birthright.' Without such an institution the integrity of the Faith would be imperiled, and the stability of the entire fabric would be gravely endangered. Its prestige would suffer, the means required to enable it to take a long, an uninterrupted view over a series of generations would be completely lacking, and the necessary guidance to define the sphere of the legislative action of its elected representatives would be totally withdrawn."

("The Dispensation of Bahá'u'lláh,"
The World Order of Bahá'u'lláh, p. 148)

Let the friends who wish for a clearer understanding of this passage at the present time consider it in the light of the many other texts which deal with the same subject, for example the following passages gleaned from the letters of Shoghi Effendi:

"They have also, in unequivocal and emphatic language, appointed those twin institutions of the House of Justice and of the Guardianship as their chosen successors, destined to apply the principles, promulgate the laws, protect the institutions, adapt loyally and intelligently the Faith to the requirements of progressive society, and consummate the incorruptible inheritance which the Founders of the Faith have bequeathed to the world."

(Letter dated 21st March 1930,
The World Order of Bahá'u'lláh, p. 20)

"It must be also clearly understood by every believer that the institution of Guardianship does not under any circumstances abrogate, or even in the slightest degree detract from, the powers granted to the Universal House of Justice by Bahá'u'lláh in the Kitáb-i-Aqdas, and repeatedly and solemnly confirmed by 'Abdu'l-Bahá in His Will. It does not constitute in any manner a contradiction to the Will and Writings of Bahá'u'lláh, nor does it nullify any of His revealed instructions. It enhances the prestige of that exalted assembly, stabilizes its supreme position, safeguards its unity, assures the continuity of its labors, without presuming in the slightest to infringe upon the inviolability of its clearly defined sphere of jurisdiction. We stand indeed too close to so monumental a document to claim for ourselves a complete understanding of all its implications, or to presume to have grasped the manifold mysteries it undoubtedly contains."

(Letter dated 27th February 1929,
The World Order of Bahá'u'lláh, p. 8)

"From these statements it is made indubitably clear and evident that the Guardian of the Faith has been made the Interpreter of the Word and that the Universal House of Justice has been invested with the function of legislating on matters not expressly revealed in the teachings. The interpretation of the Guardian, functioning within his own sphere, is as authoritative and binding as the enactments of the International House of Justice, whose exclusive right and prerogative is to pronounce upon and deliver the final judgment on such laws and ordinances as Bahá'u'lláh has not expressly revealed. Neither can, nor will ever, infringe upon the sacred and prescribed domain of the other. Neither will seek to curtail the specific and undoubted authority with which both have been divinely invested."

("The Dispensation of Bahá'u'lláh," *The World Order of Bahá'u'lláh*, p. 150)

"Each exercises, within the limitations imposed upon it, its powers, its authority, its rights and prerogatives. These are neither contradictory, nor detract in the slightest degree from the position which each of these institutions occupies."

("The Dispensation of Bahá'u'lláh," *The World Order of Bahá'u'lláh*, p. 148)

"Though the Guardian of the Faith has been made the permanent head of so august a body he can never, even temporarily, assume the right of exclusive legislation. He cannot override the decision of the majority of his fellow members. . . ."

("The Dispensation of Bahá'u'lláh," *The World Order of Bahá'u'lláh*, p. 150)

Above all, let the hearts of the friends be assured by these words of Bahá'u'lláh:

"The Hand of Omnipotence hath established His Revelation upon an unassailable, an enduring foundation. Storms of human strife are powerless to undermine its basis, nor will men's fanciful theories succeed in damaging its structure."

(Quoted on p. 109 of
The World Order of Bahá'u'lláh)

and these of 'Abdu'l-Bahá:

"Verily, God effecteth that which He pleaseth; naught can annul His Covenant; naught can obstruct His favor nor oppose His Cause! He doeth with His will that which pleaseth Him and He is powerful over all things!"

(*Tablets of 'Abdu'l-Bahá*,
Vol. III p. 598)

It should be understood by the friends that before legislating upon any matter the Universal House of Justice studies carefully and exhaustively both the Sacred Texts and the writings of Shoghi Effendi on the subject. The interpretations written by the beloved Guardian cover a vast range of subjects and are equally as binding as the Text itself.

There is a profound difference between the interpretations of the Guardian and the elucidations of the House of Justice in exercise of its function to "deliberate upon all problems which have caused difference, questions that are obscure, and matters that are not expressly recorded in the Book." The Guardian reveals what the Scripture means; his interpretation is a statement of truth which cannot be varied. Upon the Universal House of Justice, in the words of the Guardian, "has been conferred the exclusive right of legislating on matters not expressly revealed in the Bahá'í Writings." Its pronouncements, which are susceptible of amendment or abrogation by the House of Justice itself, serve to supplement and apply the Law of God. Although not invested with the function of interpretation, the House

Unassailable Foundation of the Cause of God

of Justice is in a position to do everything necessary to establish the World Order of Bahá'u'lláh on this earth. Unity of doctrine is maintained by the existence of the authentic texts of Scripture and the voluminous interpretations of 'Abdu'l-Bahá and Shoghi Effendi, together with the absolute prohibition against anyone propounding "authoritative" or "inspired" interpretations or usurping the function of Guardian. Unity of administration is assured by the authority of the Universal House of Justice.

"Such," in the words of Shoghi Effendi, "is the immutability of His revealed Word. Such is the elasticity which characterizes the functions of His appointed ministers. The first preserves the identity of His Faith, and guards the integrity of His law. The second enables it, even as a living organism, to expand and adapt itself to the needs and requirements of an ever-changing society."

(Letter dated 21st March 1930,
The World Order of Bahá'u'lláh, p. 23)

Every true believer, if he is to deepen in his understanding of the Cause of Bahá'u'lláh, must needs combine profound faith in the unfailing efficacy of His Message and His Covenant with the humility of recognizing that no one of this generation can claim to have embraced the vastness of His Cause nor to have comprehended the manifold mysteries and potentialities it contains. The words of Shoghi Effendi bear ample testimony to this fact:

"How vast is the Revelation of Bahá'u'lláh! How great the magnitude of His blessings showered upon humanity in this day! And yet, how poor, how inadequate our conception of their significance and glory! This generation stands too close to so colossal a Revelation to appreciate, in their full measure, the infinite possibilities of His Faith, the unprecedented character of His Cause, and the mysterious dispensations of His Providence."

(Letter dated 21st March 1930,
The World Order of Bahá'u'lláh, p. 24)

"We are called upon by our beloved Master in His Will and Testament not only to adopt it (Bahá'u'lláh's new World Order) unreservedly, but to unveil its merit to all the world. To attempt to estimate its full value and grasp its exact significance after so short a time since its inception would be premature and presumptuous on our part. We must trust to time, and the guidance of God's Universal House of Justice, to obtain a clearer and fuller understanding of its provisions and implications."

(Letter dated 23rd February 1924,
Bahá'í Administration, p. 62)

"As to the order and the management of the spiritual affairs of the friends, that which is very important now is the consolidation of the spiritual assemblies in every center, because, on these fortified and unshakable foundations, God's Supreme House of Justice shall be erected and firmly established in the days to come. When this most great Edifice shall be reared on such an immovable foundation, God's purpose, wisdom, universal truths, mysteries, and realities of the Kingdom, which the mystic Revelation of Bahá'u'lláh has deposited within the Will and Testament of 'Abdu'l-Bahá, shall gradually be revealed and made manifest."

(Letter in Persian, dated 19th December 1922)

Statements such as these indicate that the full meaning of the Will and Testament of 'Abdu'l-Bahá, as well as an understanding of the implications of the World Order

Unassailable Foundation of the Cause of God

ushered in by that remarkable Document, can be revealed only gradually to men's eyes, and after the Universal House of Justice has come into being. The friends are called upon to trust to time and to await the guidance of the Universal House of Justice, which, as circumstances require, will make pronouncements that will resolve and clarify obscure matters.

The Authority to Expel

The third group of queries raised by the friends concerns details of functioning of the Universal House of Justice in the absence of the Guardian, particularly the matter of expulsion of members of the House of Justice. Such questions will be clarified in the constitution of the House of Justice, the formulation of which is a goal of the Nine Year Plan. Meanwhile the friends are informed that any member committing a "sin injurious to the common weal" may be expelled from membership of the House of Justice by a majority vote of the House itself. Should any member, God forbid, be guilty of breaking the Covenant, the matter would be investigated by the Hands of the Cause of God, and the Covenant-breaker would be expelled by decision of the Hands of the Cause of God residing in the Holy Land, subject to the approval of the House of Justice, as in the case of any other believer. The decision of the Hands in such a case would be announced to the Bahá'í world by the Universal House of Justice.

We are certain that when you share this letter with the friends and they have these quotations from the Scriptures and the writings of the Guardian drawn to their attention, their doubts and misgivings will be dispelled and they will be able to devote their every effort to spreading the Message of Bahá'u'lláh, serenely confident in the power of His Covenant to overcome whatever tests an inscrutable Providence may shower upon it, thus demonstrating its ability to redeem a travailing world and to upraise the Standard of the Kingdom of God on earth.

[March 9, 1965]

Majestic Process Gathering Momentum

First Year's Victories

The tide of victory which carried the Bahá'í world community to the celebrations of the Most Great Jubilee is still rising.

A ceaseless shower of divine confirmation rains upon our efforts, its evidences apparent in the many noteworthy achievements of the few brief months since the launching of the Nine Year Plan. The most spectacular of these is the increase in the number of centers where Bahá'ís reside from fifteen thousand one hundred and sixty-eight at Riḍván 1964 to twenty-one thousand and six at the present time, an increase of nearly six thousand in one year. No less remarkable is the progress of the teaching work in India where the number of believers now exceeds a hundred and forty thousand, an increase of more than thirty thousand since Riḍván 1964. Pioneers are moving to those few remaining territories of the earth as yet unillumined by the light of God's new Revelation; "the vast increase" in the size of the Cause, called for at the launching of the Plan, appears to be developing, while in country after country the institutions and endowments of the Faith are being steadily and firmly established.

During the past twelve months the goals assigned to the World Center have been actively pursued. Basic decisions and actions to implement the goal of "Development of the institution of the Hands of the Cause of God, with a view to extension into the future of its appointed functions of protection and propagation," have already been conveyed to the friends. Following their meeting in the Holy Land last October, the members of this august body, the standard bearers of this Nine Year Plan as well as of the beloved Guardian's Ten Year Crusade, already laden with honors and services, have arisen with renewed and matchless vigor to rouse the spirits of the friends to meet the supreme teaching challenge, to lend their counsel and assistance to the administrative bodies, and to diffuse the divine fragrances and love of God through all the world. The increase in the numbers of Board members and the new executive arrangements will, it is confidently anticipated, enable the beloved Hands to discharge their important duties with even greater effectiveness and give them more time to travel and teach.

A preliminary survey of the conditions affecting the construction of the first Mashriqu'l-Adhkár of Latin America, one of the two edifices to be erected during the Plan, has already been undertaken, and we now invite Bahá'í and non-Bahá'í architects to submit designs for the Panama Temple. The terms and conditions of the submission, and the specifications of the structure, may be obtained from the National Spiritual Assembly of Panama, whose choice of design will be subject to the ultimate approval of the Universal House of Justice. It is our hope that the construction of this sacred House of Worship, in a location accorded such special significance by both the Master and the Guardian, will be speedily accomplished, so that its beacon of spiritual light may radiate to all the Americas.

During the past twelve months the following new territories have been opened to the Faith: in the continent of Africa, Gabon, Ifni, Mali, Mauritania, Rodrigues Island, and Upper Volta; in the continent of America, Aruba Island, Cozumel Island, Guadeloupe, Las Mujeres Island, Prince of Wales Island, and St. Vincent; in the continent of Asia, the Ryukyu Islands; in the continent of Australasia, the Line Islands; in the continent of Europe, the Isle of Wight, the East and West Frisian Islands. The following territories have been reopened: in the continent of Africa, Mafia Island; in the continent of America, Antigua, French Guiana, and Martinique; West Irian in the continent of Asia; and Admiralty Islands in Australasia. National Ḥaẓíratu'l-Quds have been acquired in nine places, the seats of national spiritual assemblies, and land has been acquired in two others on which to build this institution. Six national spiritual assemblies have become incorporated and the Faith has been recognized in Cambodia, a country destined to have its own national spiritual assembly during the Nine Year Plan. National endowments have been acquired in eight countries; six teaching institutes have been established, and land has been acquired for six others; a Bahá'í Publishing Trust for the provision of literature in the French language has been established in Brussels; Bahá'í holy days have been recognized in three territories; Bahá'í literature has been published in the following eleven new languages: Ibibio-Efik in the continent of Africa, Aguacateca, Athebascan, Cariña, and Motilon-Yukpa in the continent of America, Kenyah, Melanau, and Temiar in the continent of Asia, and Ghari, Marshallese, and Motua in Australasia. The progress of the Cause in Borneo makes possible the achievement of a goal supplementary to the Plan, namely the establishment at Riḍván 1966 of the National Spiritual Assembly of the Bahá'ís of Brunei.

Two Conditions in Bahá'í World Community

The passage of the first year of the Plan discloses two conditions in the Bahá'í world community. The first, within the Faith itself, is its capacity to accomplish all and any definitive goals assigned to it, goals such as the purchasing of Ḥaẓíratu'l-Quds, Temple sites, endowments, or the incorporation of spiritual assemblies; such objective and highly important goals as these, by which the Cause is established physically, legally, and socially in the world, are now taken in its stride by the Administrative Order. It should be noted, moreover, that the accomplishment of many goals of this type involves interassembly cooperation, an international activity vital to the development of world order.

The second condition apparent after the passage of the first year of the Plan involves the relationship of the Cause to humanity. Almost universally there is a sense of an impending breakthrough in large-scale conversion. Reports of the Hands of the Cause and of Board members constantly mention it; many national spiritual assemblies believe that they have reached the shores of this ocean. And, indeed, entry into the Cause by troops has been a fact in some areas for a number of years. But greater things are ahead. The teaching of the Faith must enkindle a world-encircling fire in whose light the Cause and the world—protagonists of the greatest drama in human history—are clearly illumined. Destiny is carrying us to this climax; we must gird ourselves for heroism.

Dispatch of Four Hundred Sixty Pioneers

Four challenging and immediate tasks present themselves. The first is to raise and dispatch, during the coming year, no less than four hundred and sixty pioneers who will open the fifty-four remaining virgin territories of the Plan, resettle the eighteen unoccupied ones, reinforce areas where the numbers and cohesion of the Bahá'í communities are at present inadequate to launch effective teaching plans, and support and extend the work in the areas of mass teaching. Let every believer consider this challenge, be he, in the words of the beloved Guardian, "in active service or not,

Majestic Process Gathering Momentum

of either sex, young as well as old, rich or poor, whether veteran or newly enrolled . . ."

To assist the pioneer efforts of the friends and their transfer to their posts during the next twelve months we announce the formation of five continental pioneer committees, namely: Pioneer Committee for Africa appointed by the National Spiritual Assembly of the Bahá'ís of the British Isles; Pioneer Committee for the Americas appointed by the National Spiritual Assembly of the Bahá'ís of the United States; Pioneer Committee for Asia appointed by the National Spiritual Assembly of the Bahá'ís of Persia; Pioneer Committee for Australasia appointed by the National Spiritual Assembly of the Bahá'ís of Australia; Pioneer Committee for Europe appointed by the National Spiritual Assembly of the Bahá'ís of Germany.

These committees will in no way infringe upon the responsibilities of other pioneer committees, or of national spiritual assemblies, who are in charge of the teaching work, and under whose jurisdiction they will function. They are established to facilitate and assist the work of these national bodies by providing effective exchange of vital information, both continentally and intercontinentally, by assisting in the routing of pioneer offers, and in the transfer of pioneers to their posts.

A careful estimate has been made of the pioneer needs of every area during the next twelve months and the result, including those for the seventy-two areas mentioned above, is a call for four hundred and sixty-one pioneers; eighty-six for Africa, ninety-six for the Americas, one hundred and ninety-one for Asia, twenty-nine for Australasia, and fifty-nine for Europe. Each national spiritual assembly has been consulted as to its pioneer needs and these have been made known to all national spiritual assemblies as well as to the five continental pioneer committees, who will be kept currently informed of progress by the national spiritual assemblies. The friends, therefore, are urged to consult their national spiritual assemblies for information about pioneer needs and responsibilities both of their own communities and in general.

For the first time in Bahá'í history, an International Deputization Fund has been established at the World Center under the administration of the Universal House of Justice. From it supplementary support will be given to specific pioneering projects when other funds are not available. All friends, and particularly those who are unable to respond to the pioneer call, are invited to support this Fund, mindful of the injunction of Bahá'u'lláh, "Center your energies in the propagation of the Faith of God. Whoso is worthy of so high a calling, let him arise and promote it. Whoso is unable, it is his duty to appoint him who will, in his stead, proclaim this Revelation, Whose power hath caused the foundation of the mightiest structures to quake, every mountain to be crushed into dust, and every soul to be dumbfounded."

Rapid Increase in Members and Institutions

The second challenge facing us is to raise the intensity of teaching to a pitch never before attained, in order to realize that "vast increase" called for in the Plan. Universal participation and constant action will win this goal. Every believer has a part to play, and is capable of playing it, for every soul meets others, and, as promised by Bahá'u'lláh, "Whosoever arises to aid Our Cause, God will render him victorious. . . ." The confusion of the world is not diminishing, rather does it increase with each passing day, and men and women are losing faith in human remedies. Realization is at last dawning that "there is no place to flee to"

Majestic Process Gathering Momentum

save God. Now is the golden opportunity; people are willing, in many places eager, to listen to the divine remedy.

The third challenge is to acquire as rapidly as possible all the remaining national Ḥaẓíratu'l-Quds, Temple sites, national endowments, and teaching institutes called for in the Plan. The speedy conclusion of these projects will save tremendous expense later and endow the Faith with increasingly valuable properties. These basic possessions are the embryos of mighty institutions of the future, but it is this generation, which, for its own protection and as its gift to posterity, must acquire them. We call upon the national spiritual assemblies charged with responsibility in this field to accord it high priority. A further, but equally important, consideration is that the achievement of this goal in the early years of the Plan will liberate the energies and resources of the growing world community for a concentrated, resolute, and relentless pursuit in its later stages of great victories whose foundations are now being laid.

Centenary of Proclamation to Kings in 1867

The fourth challenge is to prepare national and local plans for the befitting celebration of the centenary of Bahá'u'lláh's Proclamation of His Message in September/October, 1867, to the kings and rulers of the world, celebrations to be followed during the remainder of the Nine Year Plan by a sustained and well-planned program of proclamation of that same Message to the generality of mankind.

A review of the historic Proclamation by Bahá'u'lláh, as described by Shoghi Effendi in *God Passes By*, reveals that its "opening notes" were "sounded during the latter part of Bahá'u'lláh's banishment to Adrianople," and that, six years later, it "closed during the early years of His incarceration in the prison-fortress of 'Akká." These "opening notes" were the mighty and awe-inspiring words addressed by Him to the kings and rulers collectively in the Súriy-i-Mulúk, "the most momentous Tablet revealed by Bahá'u'lláh." It was penned sometime during the months of September and October 1867, and was followed by "Tablets unnumbered . . . in which the implications of His newly asserted claims were fully expounded." "Kings and emperors, severally and collectively; the chief magistrates of the Republics of the American continent; ministers and ambassadors; the Sovereign Pontiff himself; the Vicar of the Prophet of Islám; the royal Trustee of the Kingdom of the Hidden Imám; the monarchs of Christendom, its patriarchs, archbishops, bishops, priests, and monks; the recognized leaders of both the Sunní and Shí'ih sacerdotal orders; the high priests of the Zoroastrian religion; the philosophers, the ecclesiastical leaders, the wise men, and the inhabitants of Constantinople—that proud seat of both the Sultanate and the Caliphate; the entire company of the professed adherents of the Zoroastrian, the Jewish, the Christian, and Muslim Faiths; the people of the Bayán; the wise men of the world, its men of letters, its poets, its mystics, its tradesmen, the elected representatives of its peoples; His own countrymen;" all were "brought directly within the purview of the exhortations, the warnings, the appeals, the declarations, and the prophecies which constitute the theme of His momentous summons to the leaders of mankind . . ." "Urgent and stupendous as was this proclamation, it proved to be but a prelude to a still mightier revelation of the creative power of its Author, and to what may well rank as the most signal act of His ministry—the promulgation of the Kitáb-i-Aqdas." In this, the Most Holy Book, revealed in 1873, Bahá'u'lláh not only once more

Majestic Process Gathering Momentum 65

announces to the kings of the earth collectively that "He Who is the King of Kings hath appeared" but addresses reigning sovereigns distinctively by name and proclaims to the "rulers of America and the Presidents of the Republics therein" that "the Promised One hath appeared." Such was the Proclamation of Bahá'u'lláh to mankind. As He Himself testified, "Never since the beginning of the world hath the Message been so openly proclaimed."

The celebration of this fate-laden centenary period will open with a visit, in September 1967, on the Feast of Mashíyyat, by a few appointed representatives of the Bahá'í world to the site of the house in Adrianople, where the historic Súriy-i-Mulúk was revealed.

Immediately following this joyful and pious act, six intercontinental conferences will be simultaneously held during the month of October in Panama City, Wilmette, Sydney, Kampala, Frankfurt, and New Delhi. The host and convenor of each conference will be the national spiritual assembly in whose area it takes place. The following Hands of the Cause of God will represent the Universal House of Justice at these conferences: Panama City—Amatu'l-Bahá Rúhíyyih Khánum, who will, on that occasion, lay the foundation stone of the Temple; Wilmette—Leroy Ioas; Sydney—Ugo Giachery; Kampala—'Alí-Akbar Furútan; Frankfurt—Paul Haney; New Delhi—'Abu'l-Qásim Faizí.

All national spiritual assemblies are called upon to arrange befitting observances, on a national and local scale, of the opening of the centenary period during September/October, 1967, and between the above conferences and Riḍván 1968, at which time the second International Convention for the election of the Universal House of Justice will be held at the World Center.

The successful carrying out of all these plans will constitute a befitting commemoration, commensurate with the resources of the Bahá'í world community, of the sacred event they recall.

PERIOD OF PROCLAMATION

These six conferences, like the epoch-making event whose centenary they commemorate, will sound the "opening notes" of a period of proclamation of the Cause of God extending through the remaining years of the Nine Year Plan to the centenary, in 1973, of the revelation of the Kitáb-i-Aqdas, an activity which calls for the ardent and imaginative study of all national and local spiritual assemblies throughout the world.

The international scene will witness the holding of oceanic conferences forecast by Shoghi Effendi. The first one will be held during August 1968 on an island in the Mediterranean Sea to commemorate Bahá'u'lláh's voyage upon that sea, a hundred years before, from Gallipoli in Turkey to the Most Great Prison in 'Akká. In the subsequent years of the Nine Year Plan, others will be held in the Atlantic Ocean, in the Caribbean Sea, the Pacific Ocean, and the Indian Ocean.

In calling upon all national spiritual assemblies to consider now the appointment of national proclamation committees charged with laying feasible and effective plans for the proclamation of the Faith throughout the entire centenary period, we can do no better than call attention to the following passage from a letter written by our beloved Guardian in connection with the celebrations of the centenary of the birth of the Bahá'í Era:

"An unprecedented, a carefully conceived, efficiently coordinated nationwide campaign, aiming at the proclamation of the Message of Bahá'u'lláh, through speeches, articles in the press, and radio broadcasts, should be promptly initiated and vigorously prosecuted. The universality of the Faith, its aims and purposes, episodes in its dramatic history, testimonials to its transforming power, and the character and distinguishing features of its World Order should be emphasized and explained to the general public, and particularly to eminent friends and leaders sympathetic to its cause, who should be approached and invited to participate in the celebrations. Lectures, conferences, banquets, special publications should, to whatever extent is practicable and according to the resources at the disposal of the believers, proclaim the character of this joyous festival."

MAJESTIC PROCESS GATHERING MOMENTUM

The majestic process launched by our beloved Guardian in 1953, when he called the widely scattered, obscure Bahá'í world community to embark upon that first, glorious, world-encompassing crusade, is gathering momentum, and posterity may well gaze with awe upon the development, by so small a fraction of the human race and in a world entangled in opposition, enmity, and disruption, of the very pattern and sinews of world order. This divinely propelled and long-promised development must continue its historic course until its final consummation in the glories and splendors of the World Order of Bahá'u'lláh, the Kingdom of God on earth.

[Riḍván 1965]

Call for Pioneers

Announce all believers rejoice response Bahá'í world pioneer call raised Riḍván message requiring four hundred sixty pioneers course current year. Thus far ninety-three settled posts including fifteen virgin territories: St. Andres Island, Providencia Island, Marmara Island, Chad, Niger, Cayman Islands, Turks and Caicos, Ischia, Gotland, Alaska Peninsula, Barbuda, St. Kitts-Nevis, Inner Hebrides, Bornholm, Capri. Thirty-five additional settled same goals. One hundred sixty-seven more arisen and in process settling. Total two hundred ninety-five souls responded call. Further two hundred believers needed next four swiftly passing months fill remaining goals. Fate pioneer plan hanging balance, praying fervently holy shrines required number heroic souls arise meet challenge critical hour. Urge promptly assemblies needing funds execute assignments apply immediately International Deputization Fund. Imperative settle all territories announced Riḍván except those dependent favorable circumstances. Virgin and resettlement territories priority. Confident spirit devotion friends glorious Faith ensure brilliant victory this primary objective so vital Nine Year Plan.

[Cablegram, December 11, 1965]

Observance of Bahá'í Holy Days

From time to time questions have arisen about the application of the law of the Kitáb-i-Aqdas on the observance of Bahá'í holy days. As you know, the recognition of Bahá'í holy days in at least ninety-five countries of the world is an important and highly significant objective of the Nine Year Plan, and is directly linked with the recognition of the Faith of Bahá'u'lláh by the civil authorities as an independent religion enjoying its own rights and privileges.

The attainment of this objective will be facilitated and enhanced if the friends, motivated by their own realization of the importance of the laws of Bahá'u'lláh, are obedient to them. For the guidance of believers we repeat the instructions of the beloved Guardian:

"He wishes also to stress the fact that, according to our Bahá'í laws, work is forbidden on our nine holy days. Believers who have independent businesses or shops should refrain from working on these days. Those who are in government employ should, on religious grounds, make an effort to be excused from work; all believers, whoever their employers, should do likewise. If the government, or other employers, refuse to grant them these days off, they are not required to forfeit their employment, but they should make every effort to have the independent status of their Faith recognized and their right to hold their own religious holy days acknowledged." (*From letter written on behalf of the Guardian to the American National Spiritual Assembly, dated July 7, 1947—Bahá'í News No. 198, page 3*)

"This distinction between institutions that are under full

or partial Bahá'í control is of a fundamental importance. Institutions that are entirely managed by Bahá'ís are, for reasons that are only too obvious, under the obligation of enforcing all the laws and ordinances of the Faith, especially those whose observance constitutes a matter of conscience. There is no reason, no justification whatever, that they should act otherwise . . . The point which should be always remembered is that the issue in question is essentially a matter of conscience, and as such is of a binding effect upon all believers." (*From letter written on behalf of the Guardian to the American National Spiritual Assembly, dated October 2, 1935—Bahá'í News No. 97, page 9*)

In addition, steps should be taken to have Bahá'í children excused, on religious grounds, from attending school on Bahá'í holy days wherever possible. The Guardian has said:

"Regarding children: at fifteen a Bahá'í is of age as far as keeping the laws of the Aqdas is concerned—prayer, fasting, etc. But children under fifteen should certainly observe the Bahá'í holy days, and not go to school, if this can be arranged on these nine days." (*From letter written on behalf of the Guardian, dated October 25, 1947, to the American National Spiritual Assembly*)

National assemblies should give this subject their careful consideration, and should provide ways and means for bringing this matter to the attention of the believers under their jurisdiction so that, as a matter of conscience, the mass of believers will uphold these laws and observe them.

[28 January, 1966]*

Arming for Third Phase of the Nine Year Plan

The fiftieth anniversary of the revelation by 'Abdu'l-Bahá, in March and April 1916, of the first Tablets of the Divine Plan, has witnessed the conclusion of a feat of pioneering unparalleled in the annals of the Cause. A year ago the call was raised for four hundred and sixty-one pioneers to leave their homes within twelve months and scatter throughout the planet to broaden and strengthen the foundations of the world community of Bahá'u'lláh. There is every hope that, with the exception of thirty-four posts whose settlement is dependent upon favorable circumstances, all the pioneer goals will be filled by Riḍván or their settlement will be assured by firm commitments. The gratitude and admiration of the entire Bahá'í world go out to this noble band of dedicated believers who have so gloriously responded to the call. These pioneers, who have arisen for the specified goals, have been reinforced by a further forty-five believers who have settled in the goal territories, while sixty-nine more have left their homes to reside in twenty-six other countries already opened to the Faith. All told, in the course of the year, five hundred and five Bahá'ís have arisen to pioneer beyond their homelands, the largest number ever to do so in any one year in the entire history of the Cause.

RESOUNDING VICTORIES OF PAST YEAR

This is a resounding victory, and in the light of the Master's statement in the first of the Tablets of the Divine Plan, "It has often happened that one blessed soul has become the source of the guidance of a nation," of wonderful portent for the future. Its immediate results are the opening of twenty-four new territories to the Faith, the resettlement of four others, and the consolidation of ninety-three more. The newly opened territories are: Chad and Niger in Africa; Alaskan Peninsula, Barbuda, Cayman Islands, Chiloé Island, Providencia Island, Quintana Roo Territory, Saba, St. Andrés Island, St. Eustatius, St. Kitts-Nevis, St. Lawrence Island, Tierra del Fuego, and Turks and Caicos Islands in the Americas; Laccadive Islands and Marmara Island in Asia; Niue Island in Australasia; and Bornholm, Capri, Elba, Gotland, Inner Hebrides, and Ischia in Europe.

The resettled territories are: Corisco Island and Spanish Guinea in Africa, and Maldive Islands and Nicobar Islands in Asia.

As announced last Riḍván, the first Convention of the Bahá'ís of Brunei will be held this year, during the second weekend of the Riḍván period, when the first National Spiritual Assembly of the Bahá'ís of Brunei will be elected. Hand of the Cause Collis Featherstone will represent the World Center of the Faith on this historic occasion.

NINE NEW NATIONAL ASSEMBLIES IN RIḌVÁN 1967

A further result of the confirmations which have rewarded the tremendous teaching effort of the past two years is the call now made by the House of Justice for the formation at Riḍván 1967 of the following nine national spiritual assemblies: In Africa—the National Spiritual Assembly of Algeria and Tunisia with its seat in Algiers; the National Spiritual Assembly of Cameroon Republic with its seat in Victoria and with Spanish Guinea, Fernando Po, Corisco, and São Tomé and Príncipe Islands assigned to it; the National Spiritual Assembly of Swaziland, Mozambique, and Basutoland with its seat in Mbabane; the National Spiritual

Assembly of Zambia with its seat in Lusaka. In the Americas—the National Spiritual Assembly of the Leeward, Windward, and Virgin Islands with its seat in Charlotte Amalie. In Asia—the National Spiritual Assembly of Cambodia with its seat in Phnom Penh; the National Spiritual Assembly of Eastern and Southern Arabia with its seat in Baḥrayn; the National Spiritual Assembly of Taiwan with its seat in Taipei. In Australasia—the National Spiritual Assembly of the Gilbert and Ellice Islands with its seat in Tarawa. These nine new national spiritual assemblies constituting, together with the new National Spiritual Assembly of Brunei, ten additional pillars of the Universal House of Justice, will bring to seventy-nine the number which will take part during Riḍván 1968 in the second International Convention for the election of that institution.

This momentous year cannot be allowed to pass without mention of the tireless and dedicated services of the beloved Hands of the Cause, the standard bearers of the Nine Year Plan, and the able support rendered them by their Auxiliary Boards. The special missions which they have discharged on behalf of the Universal House of Justice, the teaching tours they have undertaken, the conferences they have organized, their constant work at the World Center, and above all their never-ending encouragement of the friends and watchfulness over the welfare of the Cause of God, have given distinction and effective leadership to the work of the entire community. The grievous loss which they sustained in the passing of Hand of the Cause Leroy Ioas is shared by the whole Bahá'í world.

Three-fold Purpose of Intercontinental Conferences

The splendid achievements in the pioneering and teaching fields, together with the enthusiastic attention given to the preparation of plans for the befitting celebration of the centenary of Bahá'u'lláh's Proclamation of His Message to the kings and rulers of the world, have sealed with success the first, and opened the way for the second phase of the Nine Year Plan, a phase in which the Bahá'í world must prepare and arm itself for the third phase, beginning in October 1967 when the six intercontinental conferences will sound the "opening notes" of a period of proclamation of the Cause of God extending through the remaining years of the Nine Year Plan to the centenary, in 1973, of the revelation of the Kitáb-i-Aqdas. The three-fold purpose of these conferences is to commemorate the centenary of the opening of Bahá'u'lláh's own Proclamation of His Mission, to proclaim the Divine Message, and to deliberate upon the tasks of the remaining years of the Nine Year Plan.

Tasks of Second Phase of Nine Year Plan

Five specific tasks face the Bahá'í world as it enters this second phase of the Plan:

The first is to complete the settlement of the pioneers, and the dispatch of others wherever needed.

The second is intensive preparation for the third phase of the Plan through development of new teaching measures and expansion of the various Bahá'í funds at international, national, and local levels.

The third is acceleration of the provision of Bahá'í literature, particularly its translation and publication in those languages in which, as yet, none has been published or the supply is inadequate.

The fourth is the acquisition of the remaining national Ḥaẓíratu'l-Quds, Temple sites, national endowments, and teaching institutes called for in the Plan, before the developing inflation now affecting nearly the whole world adds too greatly to the financial burden of acquiring these properties.

Arming for Third Phase of the Nine Year Plan

The fifth is development of the Panama Temple Fund. The Universal House of Justice is initiating this Fund with a contribution of $25,000, and now calls upon the believers and Bahá'í communities to contribute liberally and continuously until the funds for the completion of this historic structure are assured. Such contributions should be sent directly to the National Spiritual Assembly of Panama. More than fifty designs have been received, and the House of Justice is now considering the recommendations of the National Assembly. The choice will be announced and the friends will be kept fully informed of the progress of this highly significant and inspiring project.

CHALLENGE TO EVERY MEMBER AND INSTITUTION

Every individual follower of Bahá'u'lláh, as well as the institutions of the Faith, at local, national, continental, and world levels, must now meet the challenge to raise the intensity of teaching to a pitch never before attained, in order to realize that vast increase called for in the Plan. For those believers living in countries where they have freedom to teach their Faith, this challenge is the more sharply pointed by the oppressive measures imposed on the Faith elsewhere. In Persia the believers are denied their elementary rights and the Faith is still largely proscribed. In 'Iráq the national and one local Ḥaẓíratu'l-Quds have been seized and the activities of the friends severely restricted. In Egypt Bahá'í properties are still confiscated and recently several believers were imprisoned for a period, and are now awaiting trial. New oppression has broken out in Indonesia where the national Ḥaẓíratu'l-Quds has been seized and organized activities of the believers have been forbidden. In yet other countries the believers are subject to restrictions and surveillance. The friends in all cases are steadfast and confident, looking forward to their emancipation and the eventual triumph of the Cause.

The challenge to the local and national administrative institutions of the Faith is to organize and promote the teaching work through systematic plans, involving not only the regular fireside meetings in the homes of the believers, the public meetings, receptions, and conferences, the week-end, summer, and winter schools, the youth conferences and activities, all of which are so vigorously upheld at present, but in addition through a constant stream of visiting teachers to every locality. The forces released by this latter process have been extolled by Bahá'u'lláh in these words:

> "The movement itself from place to place when undertaken for the sake of God hath always exerted, and can now exert, its influence in the world. In the Books of old the station of them that have voyaged far and near in order to guide the servants of God hath been set forth and written down."

while 'Abdu'l-Bahá, in the Tablets of the Divine Plan, says:

> "Teachers must continually travel to all parts of the continent, nay, rather, to all parts of the world . . ."

Such plans must be initiated and developed now, during this period of preparation, so that they may be fully operative by the beginning of the proclamation period from which time they must be relentlessly pursued until the end of the Plan.

The Call for Traveling Teachers

The Universal House of Justice attaches such importance to this principle of traveling teaching that it has decided to develop it internationally, and now calls for volunteers to offer their services in this field. By their visits to lands other than their own, these friends will lend a tremendous stimulus to the proclamation and teaching of the Cause in all continents. It is hoped that such projects will be self-supporting, since the International Deputization Fund will still be needed for pioneering. However, when a proposal which is considered to be of special benefit to the Faith cannot be financed by the individual or the receiving national assemblies, the House of Justice will consider a request for assistance from the Deputization Fund. Offers, which may be for any period, should be made to one's own national spiritual assembly or to the continental pioneer committees, which have been given the additional task of assisting national assemblies to implement and coordinate this new enterprise. Let those who arise recall the Master's injunction to "travel like 'Abdu'l-Bahá . . . sanctified and free from every attachment and in the utmost severance."

EXPANSION AND CONSOLIDATION ARE COEQUAL

Simultaneous and coequal with this vast, ordered, and ever-growing teaching effort, the work of consolidation must go hand in hand. In fact these two processes must be regarded as inseparable parts of the expansion of the Faith. While the work of teaching inevitably goes first, to pursue it alone without consolidation would leave the community unprepared to receive the masses who must sooner or later respond to the life-giving message of the Cause. The guidance of our beloved Guardian in this vital matter is, as ever, clear and unambiguous: "Every outward thrust into new fields, every multiplication of Bahá'í institutions, must be paralleled by a deeper thrust of the roots which sustain the spiritual life of the community and ensure its sound development. From this vital, this ever-present need attention must, at no time, be diverted, nor must it be, under any circumstances, neglected, or subordinated to the no less vital and urgent task of ensuring the outer expansion of

Bahá'í administrative institutions." A proper balance between these two essential aspects of its development must, from now on, as we enter the era of large-scale conversion, be maintained by the Bahá'í community. Consolidation must comprise not only the establishment of Bahá'í administrative institutions, but a true deepening in the fundamental verities of the Cause and in its spiritual principles, understanding of its prime purpose in the establishment of the unity of mankind, instruction in its standards of behavior in all aspects of private and public life, in the particular practice of Bahá'í life in such things as daily prayer, education of children, observance of the laws of Bahá'í marriage, abstention from politics, the obligation to contribute to the Fund, the importance of the Nineteen Day Feast, and opportunity to acquire a sound knowledge of the present-day practice of Bahá'í administration.

URGENT NEED FOR INCREASED FLOW OF FUNDS

The onward march of the Faith requires, and is indeed dependent upon, a very great increase in contributions to the various funds. All the goals assigned to the World Center of the Faith, and particularly those dealing with the development and beautification of the properties surrounding the holy shrines and the extension of the gardens on Mount Carmel, entail heavy expenditures. The building of the two Temples called for in the Plan will require further large sums, and the worldwide process of teaching and consolidation now to be intensified must be sustained by a greatly increased and uninterrupted flow of funds. The International Deputization Fund must be maintained and expanded, not only for further pioneering needs, but in order to assist and develop the traveling teacher program now called for. Since only those who have openly proclaimed their recognition of Bahá'u'lláh are permitted to contribute financially to the establishment of His World Order, it is apparent that more, much more, is required from the few now so privileged. Our responsibilities in this field are very great, commensurate indeed with the bounty of being the bearers of the Name of God in this Day.

The challenge to the individual Bahá'í in every field of service, but above all in teaching the Cause of God, is never-ending. With every fresh affliction visited upon mankind our inescapable duty becomes more apparent, nor should we ever forget that if we neglect this duty, "others," in the words of Shoghi Effendi, "will be called upon to take up our task as ministers to the crying needs of this afflicted world." Now, it seems, we may well be entering an era of the longed-for expansion of our beloved Faith. Mankind's growing hunger for spiritual truth is our opportunity. While reaching forth to grasp it, we would do well to ponder the following words of Bahá'u'lláh:

"Your behavior towards your neighbor should be such as to manifest clearly the signs of the one true God, for ye are the first among men to be recreated by His Spirit, the first to adore and bow the knee before Him, the first to circle round His throne of Glory."

As humanity plunges deeper into that condition of which Bahá'u'lláh wrote, "to disclose it now would not be meet and seemly," so must the believers increasingly stand out as assured, orientated, and fundamentally happy beings, conforming to a standard which, in direct contrast to the ignoble and amoral attitudes of modern society, is the source of their honor, strength, and maturity. It is this marked contrast between the vigor, unity, and discipline of the Bahá'í community on the one hand, and the increasing confusion, despair, and feverish tempo of a doomed society on the other, which, during the turbulent years ahead, will draw the eyes of humanity to the sanctuary of Bahá'u'lláh's world-redeeming Faith.

The constant progress of the Cause of God is a source of joy to us all and a stimulus to further action. But not ordinary action. Heroic deeds are now called for such as are performed only by divinely sustained and detached souls. 'Abdu'l-Bahá, the Commander of the hosts of the Lord, in one of the Tablets of the Divine Plan, uttered this cry: "Oh! that I could travel, even though on foot and in the utmost poverty, to these regions and, raising the call of Yá Bahá'u'l-Abhá in cities, villages, mountains, deserts, and oceans, promote the Divine Teachings. This, alas, I cannot do. How intensely I deplore it." And He concluded with this heart-shaking appeal, "Please God, ye may achieve it."

[Riḍván 1966]

The Guardianship and the Universal House of Justice

[*Passages from a letter written in response to questions asked by an individual believer on the relationship between the Guardianship and the Universal House of Justice.*]

. . . You query the timing of the election of the Universal House of Justice in view of the Guardian's statement: ". . . given favorable circumstances under which the Bahá'ís of Persia and the adjoining countries under Soviet rule may be enabled to elect their national representatives . . . the only remaining obstacle in the way of the definite formation of the International House of Justice will have been removed." On April 19, 1947 the Guardian, in a letter written on his behalf by his secretary, replied to the inquiry of an individual believer about this passage: "At the time he referred to Russia there were Bahá'ís there. Now the community has practically ceased to exist; therefore the formation of the International House of Justice cannot depend on a Russian national spiritual assembly, but other strong national spiritual assemblies will have to be built up before it can be established."

You suggest the possibility that, for the good of the Cause, certain information concerning the succession to Shoghi Effendi is being withheld from the believers. We assure you that nothing whatsoever is being withheld from the friends for whatever reason. There is no doubt at all that in the Will and Testament of 'Abdu'l-Bahá, Shoghi Effendi was the authority designated to appoint his successor; but he had no children and all the surviving Aghṣán had broken the Covenant. Thus, as the Hands of the Cause stated in 1957, it is clear that there was no one he could have appointed in accordance with the provisions of the Will. To have made an appointment outside the clear and specific provisions of the Master's Will and Testament would obviously have been an impossible and unthinkable course of action for the Guardian, the divinely appointed upholder and defender of the Covenant. Moreover, that same Will had provided a clear means for the confirmation of the Guardian's appointment of his successor, as you are aware. The nine Hands to be elected by the body of the Hands were to give their assent by secret ballot to the Guardian's choice. In 1957 the entire body of the Hands, after fully investigating the matter, announced that Shoghi Effendi had appointed no successor and left no will. This is documented and established.

The fact that Shoghi Effendi did not leave a will cannot be adduced as evidence of his failure to obey Bahá'u'lláh—rather should we acknowledge that in his very silence there is a wisdom and a sign of his infallible guidance. We should ponder deeply the writings that we have, and seek to understand the multitudinous significances that they contain. Do not forget that Shoghi Effendi said two things were necessary for a growing understanding of the World Order of Bahá'u'lláh: the passage of time and the guidance of the Universal House of Justice.

The Infallibility of the Universal House of Justice Within Its Ordained Sphere

The infallibility of the Universal House of Justice, operating within its ordained sphere, has not been made dependent upon the presence in its membership of the Guardian of the Cause. Although in the realm of interpretation the Guardian's pronouncements are always binding, in the area of the Guardian's participation in legislation it is always the decision of the House itself which must prevail. This is supported by the words of the Guardian: "The interpretation of the Guardian, functioning within his own sphere, is as authoritative and binding as the enactments of the International House of Justice, whose exclusive right and prerogative is to pronounce upon and deliver the final judgment on such laws and ordinances as Bahá'u'lláh has not expressly revealed. Neither can, nor will ever, infringe upon the sacred and prescribed domain of the other. Neither will seek to curtail the specific and undoubted authority with which both have been divinely invested.

"Though the Guardian of the Faith has been made the permanent head of so august a body he can never, even temporarily, assume the right of exclusive legislation. He cannot override the decision of the majority of his fellow members, but is bound to insist upon a reconsideration by them of any enactment he conscientiously believes to conflict with the meaning and to depart from the spirit of Bahá'u'lláh's revealed utterances."

However, quite apart from his function as a member and sacred head for life of the Universal House of Justice, the Guardian, functioning within his own sphere, had the right and duty "to define the sphere of the legislative action" of the Universal House of Justice. In other words, he had the authority to state whether a matter was or was not already covered by the Sacred Texts and therefore whether it was within the authority of the Universal House of Justice to legislate upon it. No other person, apart from the Guardian, has the right or authority to make such definitions. The question therefore arises: In the absence of the Guardian, is the Universal House of Justice in danger of straying outside its proper sphere and thus falling into error? Here we must remember three things: First, Shoghi Effendi, during the thirty-six years of his Guardianship, has already made innumerable such definitions, supplementing those made by 'Abdu'l-Bahá and by Bahá'u'lláh Himself. As already announced to the friends, a careful study of the Writings and interpretations on any subject on which the House of Justice proposes to legislate always precedes its act of legislation. Second, the Universal House of Justice, itself assured of Divine guidance, is well aware of the absence of the Guardian and will approach all matters of legislation only when certain of its sphere of jurisdiction, a sphere which the Guardian has confidently described as "clearly defined." Third, we must not forget the Guardian's written statement about these two institutions: "Neither can, nor will ever, infringe upon the sacred and prescribed domain of the other."

Enactments of Universal House of Justice Are Inspired and Spiritual

As regards the need to have deductions made from the Writings to help in the formulation of the enactments of the House of Justice, there is the following text from the pen of 'Abdu'l-Bahá:

"Those matters of major importance which constitute the foundation of the Law of God are explicitly recorded in the Text, but subsidiary laws are left to the House of Justice. The wisdom of this is that the times never remain the same, for change is a necessary quality and an essential attribute of this world, and of time and place. Therefore the House of Justice will take action accordingly.

"Let it not be imagined that the House of Justice will take any decision according to its own concepts and opinions. God forbid! The Supreme House of Justice will take decisions and establish laws through the inspiration and confirmation of the Holy Spirit, because it is in the safekeeping and under the shelter and protection of the Ancient Beauty, and obedience to its decisions is a bounden and essential duty and an absolute obligation, and there is no escape for anyone.

"Say, O People: Verily the Supreme House of Justice is under the wings of your Lord, the Compassionate, the All-Merciful, that is under His protection, His care, and His shelter; for He has commanded the firm believers to obey that blessed, sanctified, and all-subduing body, whose sovereignty is divinely ordained and of the Kingdom of Heaven and whose laws are inspired and spiritual.

"Briefly, this is the wisdom of referring the laws of society to the House of Justice. In the religion of Islám, similarly, not every ordinance was explicitly revealed; nay not a tenth part of a tenth part was included in the Text; although all matters of major importance were specifically referred to, there were undoubtedly thousands of laws which were unspecified. These were devised by the divines of a later age according to the laws of Islamic jurisprudence, and individual divines made conflicting deductions from the original revealed ordinances. All these were enforced. Today this process of deduction is the right of the body of the House of Justice, and the deductions and conclusions of individual learned men have no authority, unless they are endorsed by the House of Justice. The difference is precisely this, that from the conclusions and endorsements of the body of the House of Justice whose members are elected by and known to the worldwide Bahá'í community, no differences will arise; whereas the conclusions of individual divines and scholars would definitely lead to differences, and result in schism, division, and dispersion. The oneness of the Word would be destroyed, the unity of the Faith would disappear, and the edifice of the Faith of God would be shaken."

Ensures Continuity of Authority Which Flows from the Source of Our Faith

In the Order of Bahá'u'lláh there are certain functions which are reserved to certain institutions, and others which are shared in common, even though they may be more in the special province of one or the other. For example, although the Hands of the Cause of God have the specific functions of protection and propagation, and are specialized for these functions, it is also the duty of the Universal House of Justice and the spiritual assemblies to protect and teach the Cause—indeed teaching is a sacred obligation placed upon every believer by Bahá'u'lláh. Similarly, although after the Master authoritative interpretation was exclusively vested in the Guardian, and although legislation is exclusively the function of the Universal House of Justice, these two institutions are, in Shoghi Effendi's words, "complementary in their aim and purpose." "Their common, their fundamental object is to ensure the continuity of that divinely appointed authority which flows from the Source of our Faith, to safeguard the unity of its followers, and to maintain the integrity and flexibility of its teachings." Whereas the Universal House of Justice cannot undertake any function which exclusively appertained to the Guardian, it must continue to pursue the object which it shares in common with the Guardianship.

As you point out with many quotations, Shoghi Effendi repeatedly stressed the inseparability of these two institutions. Whereas he obviously envisaged their functioning together, it cannot logically be deduced from this that one is unable to function in the absence of the other. During the whole thirty-six years of his Guardianship Shoghi Effendi functioned without the Universal House of Justice. Now the Universal House of Justice must function without the Guardian, but the principle of inseparability remains. The Guardianship does not lose its significance nor position in the Order of Bahá'u'lláh merely because there is no living Guardian. We must guard against two extremes: one is to argue that because there is no Guardian all that was written about the Guardianship and its position in the Bahá'í World Order is a dead letter and was unimportant; the other is to be so overwhelmed by the significance of the Guardianship as to underestimate the strength of the Covenant, or to be tempted to compromise with the clear Texts in order to find somehow, in some way, a "Guardian."

This Is God's Cause—Its Light Will Not Fail

Service to the Cause of God requires absolute fidelity and integrity and unwavering faith in Him. No good but only evil can come from taking the responsibility for the future of God's Cause into our own hands and trying to force it into ways that we wish it to go regardless of the clear texts and our own limitations. It is His Cause. He has promised that its light will not fail. Our part is to cling tenaciously to the revealed Word and to the institutions that He has created to preserve His Covenant.

It is precisely in this connection that the believers must recognize the importance of intellectual honesty and humility. In past dispensations many errors arose because the believers in God's Revelation were overanxious to encompass the Divine Message within the framework of their limited understanding, to define doctrines where definition was beyond their power, to explain mysteries which only the wisdom and experience of a later age would make comprehensible, to argue that something was true because it appeared desirable and necessary. Such compromises with essential truth, such intellectual pride, we must scrupulously avoid.

If some of the statements of the Universal House of Justice are not detailed the friends should realize that the cause of this is not secretiveness, but rather the determination of this body to refrain from interpreting the teachings and to preserve the truth of the Guardian's statement that "Leaders of religion, exponents of political theories, governors of human institutions . . . need have no doubt or anxiety regarding the nature, the origin, or validity of the institutions which the adherents of the Faith are building up throughout the world. For these lie embedded in the Teachings themselves, unadulterated and unobscured by unwarranted inferences or unauthorized interpretations of His Word."

Distinction Between Authoritive and Individual Interpretation

A clear distinction is made in our Faith between authoritative interpretation and the interpretation or understanding that each individual arrives at for himself from his study of its teachings. While the former is confined to the Guardian, the latter, according to the guidance given to us by the Guardian himself, should by no means be suppressed. In fact such individual interpretation is considered the fruit of man's rational power and conducive to a better understanding of the teachings, provided that no disputes or arguments arise among the friends and the individual himself understands and makes it clear that his views are merely his own. Individual interpretations continually change as one grows in comprehension of the teachings. As Shoghi Effendi wrote: "To deepen in the Cause means to read the writings of Bahá'u'lláh and the Master so thoroughly as to

Guardianship and Universal House of Justice

be able to give it to others in its pure form. There are many who have some superficial idea of what the Cause stands for. They, therefore, present it together with all sorts of ideas that are their own. As the Cause is still in its early days we must be most careful lest we fall into this error and injure the Movement we so much adore. There is no limit to the study of the Cause. The more we read the Writings, the more truths we can find in them, the more we will see that our previous notions were erroneous." So, although individual insights can be enlightening and helpful, they can also be misleading. The friends must therefore learn to listen to the views of others without being overawed or allowing their faith to be shaken, and to express their own views without pressing them on their fellow Bahá'ís.

The Cause of God is organic, growing and developing like a living being. Time and again it has faced crises which have perplexed the believers, but each time the Cause, impelled by the immutable purpose of God, overcame the crisis and went on to greater heights.

"UNTO THE MOST HOLY BOOK EVERY ONE MUST TURN"

However great may be our inability to understand the mystery and the implications of the passing of Shoghi Effendi, the strong cord to which all must cling with assurance is the Covenant. The emphatic and vigorous language of 'Abdu'l-Bahá's Will and Testament is at this time, as at the time of His own passing, the safeguard of the Cause:

> "Unto the Most Holy Book every one must turn and all that is not expressly recorded therein must be referred to the Universal House of Justice. That which this body, whether unanimously or by a majority doth carry, that is verily the truth and the purpose of God Himself. Whoso doth deviate therefrom is verily of

them that love discord, hath shown forth malice, and turned away from the Lord of the Covenant." And again: "All must seek guidance and turn unto the Center of the Cause and the House of Justice. And he that turneth unto whatsoever else is indeed in grievous error."

The Universal House of Justice, which the Guardian said would be regarded by posterity as "the last refuge of a tottering civilization," is now, in the absence of the Guardian, the sole infallibly guided institution in the world to which all must turn, and on it rests the responsibility for ensuring the unity and progress of the Cause of God in accordance with the revealed Word. There are statements from the Master and the Guardian indicating that the Universal House of Justice, in addition to being the highest legislative body of the Faith, is also the body to which all must turn, and is the "apex" of the Bahá'í Administrative Order, as well as the "supreme organ of the Bahá'í Commonwealth." The Guardian has in his writings specified for the House of Justice such fundamental functions as the formulation of future worldwide teaching plans, the conduct of the administrative affairs of the Faith, and the guidance, organization, and unification of the affairs of the Cause throughout the world. Furthermore in *God Passes By* the Guardian makes the following statement: "The Kitáb-i-Aqdas . . . not only preserves for posterity the basic laws and ordinances on which the fabric of His future World Order must rest, but ordains, in addition to the function of interpretation which it confers upon His successor, the necessary institutions through which the integrity and unity of His Faith can alone be safeguarded." He has also, in "The Dispensation of Bahá'u'lláh," written that the members of the Universal House of Justice "and not the body of those who either directly or indirectly elect them, have thus been made the recipients of the Divine guidance which is at once the lifeblood and ultimate safeguard of this Revelation."

As the Universal House of Justice has already announced, it cannot legislate to make possible the appointment of a successor to Shoghi Effendi, nor can it legislate to make possible the appointment of any more Hands of the Cause, but it must do everything within its power to ensure the performance of all those functions which it shares with these two mighty institutions. It must make provision for the proper discharge in future of the functions of protection and propagation, which the administrative bodies share with the Guardianship and the Hands of the Cause; it must, in the absence of the Guardian, receive and disburse the Ḥuqúqu'lláh, in accordance with the following statement of 'Abdu'l-Bahá: "Disposition of the Ḥuqúq, wholly or partly, is permissible, but this should be done by permission of the authority in the Cause to whom all must turn." It must make provision in its constitution for the removal of any of its members who commits a sin "injurious to the common weal." Above all, it must, with perfect faith in Bahá'u'lláh, proclaim His Cause and enforce His law so that the Most Great Peace shall be firmly established in this world and the foundation of the Kingdom of God on earth shall be accomplished.

[May 27, 1966]

Unique Opportunity in Human History

[*Letter to Bahá'í Youth in Every Land*]

In country after country the achievements of Bahá'í youth are increasingly advancing the work of the Nine Year Plan and arousing the admiration of their fellow believers. From the very beginning of the Bahá'í Era, youth have played a vital part in the promulgation of God's Revelation. The Báb Himself was but twenty-five years old when He declared His Mission, while many of the Letters of the Living were even younger. The Master, as a very young man, was called upon to shoulder heavy responsibilities in the service of His Father in 'Iráq and Turkey; and His brother, the Purest Branch, yielded up his life to God in the Most Great Prison at the age of twenty-two that the servants of God might "be quickened, and all that dwell on earth be united." Shoghi Effendi was a student at Oxford when called to the throne of his Guardianship, and many of the Knights of Bahá'u'lláh, who won imperishable fame during the Ten Year Crusade, were young people. Let it, therefore, never be imagined that youth must await their years of maturity before they can render invaluable services to the Cause of God.

A Time of Decision

For any person, whether Bahá'í or not, his youthful years are those in which he will make many decisions which will set the course of his life. In these years he is most likely to choose his life's work, complete his education, begin to earn his own living, marry, and start to raise his own family. Most important of all, it is during this period that the mind is most questing and that the spiritual values that will guide the person's future behavior are adopted. These factors present Bahá'í youth with their greatest opportunities, their greatest challenges, and their greatest tests—opportunities to truly apprehend the teachings of their Faith and to give them to their contemporaries, challenges to overcome the pressures of the world and to provide leadership for their and succeeding generations, and tests enabling them to exemplify in their lives the high moral standards set forth in the Bahá'í writings. Indeed, the Guardian wrote of the Bahá'í youth that it is they "who can contribute so decisively to the virility, the purity, and the driving force of the life of the Bahá'í community, and upon whom must depend the future orientation of its destiny, and the complete unfoldment of the potentialities with which God has endowed it."

A Critical Phase of Transition

Those who now are in their teens and twenties are faced with a special challenge and can seize an opportunity that is unique in human history. During the Ten Year Crusade —the ninth part of that majestic process described so vividly by our beloved Guardian—the community of the Most Great Name spread with the speed of lightning over the major territories and islands of the globe, increased manifoldly its manpower and resources, saw the beginning of the entry of the peoples by troops into the Cause of God, and completed the structure of the Administrative Order of Bahá'u'lláh. Now, firmly established in the world, the Cause, in the opening years of the tenth part of that same process, is perceptibly emerging from the obscurity that has, for the most part, shrouded it since its inception and is arising to challenge the outworn concepts of a corrupt society and proclaim the solution for the agonizing problems of a disordered humanity. During the lifetime of those who are now young the condition of the world, and the place of the Bahá'í Cause in it, will change immeasurably, for we are entering a highly critical phase in this era of transition.

THREE FIELDS OF SERVICE OPEN TO YOUTH

Three great fields of service lie open before young Bahá'ís, in which they will simultaneously be remaking the character of human society and preparing themselves for the work they can undertake later in their lives.

First, the foundation of all their other accomplishments, is their study of the teachings, the spiritualization of their lives, and the forming of their characters in accordance with the standards of Bahá'u'lláh. As the moral standards of the people around us collapse and decay, whether of the centuries-old civilizations of the East, the more recent cultures of Christendom and Islám, or of the rapidly changing tribal societies of the world, the Bahá'ís must increasingly stand out as pillars of righteousness and forbearance. The life of a Bahá'í will be characterized by truthfulness and decency; he will walk uprightly among his fellowmen, dependent upon none save God, yet linked by bonds of love and brotherhood with all mankind; he will be entirely detached from the loose standards, the decadent theories, the frenetic experimentation, the desperation of present-day society, will look upon his neighbors with a bright and friendly face, and be a beacon light and a haven for all those who would emulate his strength of character and assurance of soul.

The second field of service, which is linked intimately with the first, is teaching the Faith, particularly to their fellow youth, among whom are some of the most open and seeking minds in the world. Not yet having acquired all the responsibilities of a family or a long-established home and job, youth can the more easily choose where they will live and study or work. In the world at large young people travel hither and thither seeking amusement, education, and experiences. Bahá'í youth, bearing the incomparable treasure of the Word of God for this Day, can harness this mobility into service for mankind and can choose their places of residence, their areas of travel, and their types of work with the goal in mind of how they can best serve the Faith.

The third field of service is the preparation by youth for their later years. It is the obligation of a Bahá'í to educate his children; likewise it is the duty of the children to acquire knowledge of the arts and sciences and to learn a trade or a profession whereby they, in turn, can earn their living and support their families. This, for a Bahá'í youth, is in itself a service to God, a service, moreover, which can be combined with teaching the Faith and often with pioneering. The Bahá'í community will need men and women of many skills and qualifications; for, as it grows in size the sphere of its activities in the life of society will increase and diversify. Let Bahá'í youth, therefore, consider the best ways in which they can use and develop their native abilities for the service of mankind and the Cause of God, whether this be as farmers, teachers, doctors, artisans, musicians, or any one of the multitude of livelihoods that are open to them.

THE BASIS OF ALL KNOWLEDGE

When studying at school or university Bahá'í youth will often find themselves in the unusual and slightly embarrassing position of having a more profound insight into a subject than their instructors. The Teachings of Bahá'u'lláh throw light on so many aspects of human life and knowledge that a Bahá'í must learn, earlier than most, to weigh the information that is given to him rather than to accept it blindly. A Bahá'í has the advantage of the Divine Revelation for this age, which shines like a searchlight on so many problems that baffle modern thinkers; he must therefore develop the ability to learn everything from those around him, showing proper humility before his teachers, but always relating what he hears to the Bahá'í teachings, for they will enable him to sort out the gold from the dross of human error.

FUNCTION OF YOUTH WITHIN THE COMMUNITY

Paralleling the growth of his inner life through prayer, meditation, service, and study of the teachings, Bahá'í youth have the opportunity to learn in practice the very functioning of the Order of Bahá'u'lláh. Through taking part in conferences and summer schools as well as Nineteen Day Feasts, and in service on committees, they can develop the wonderful skill of Bahá'í consultation, thus tracing new paths of human corporate action. Consultation is no easy skill to learn, requiring as it does the subjugation of all egotism and unruly passions, the cultivation of frankness and freedom of thought as well as courtesy, openness of mind, and wholehearted acquiescence in a majority decision. In this field Bahá'í youth may demonstrate the efficiency, the vigor, the access of unity which arise from true consultation and, by contrast, demonstrate the futility of partisanship, lobbying, debate, secret diplomacy, and unilateral action which characterize modern affairs. Youth also take part in the life of the Bahá'í community as a whole and promote a society in which all generations—elderly, middle-aged, youth, children—are fully integrated and make up an organic whole. By refusing to carry over the antagonisms and mistrust between the generations which perplex and bedevil modern society, they will again demonstrate the healing and life-giving nature of their religion.

STEPS TO CONSIDER NOW

The Nine Year Plan has just entered its third year. The youth have already played a vital part in winning its goals. We now call upon them, with great love and highest hopes and the assurance of our fervent prayers, to consider, individually and in consultation, wherever they live and whatever their circumstances, those steps which they should take now to deepen themselves in their knowledge of the Divine Message, to develop their characters after the pattern of the Master, to acquire those skills, trades, and professions in which they can best serve God and man, to intensify their service to the Cause of Bahá'u'lláh, and to radiate its Message to the seekers among their contemporaries.

[June 10, 1966]

Three More National Assemblies To Be Formed Riḍván 1967

Joyfully announce formation at Riḍván 1967 additional new National Assemblies Belize seat Belize, Laos seat Vientiane, Sikkim seat Gangtok, calling upon National Assemblies Guatemala, Thailand, India respectively call first conventions election national assemblies. Sikkim Assembly supplementary achievement Nine Year Plan. Changed situation Cambodia requires postponement formation national assembly that country. Addition above national assemblies raises total throughout the world to eighty-one whose members will participate second International Convention. Offering prayers of gratitude Bahá'u'lláh supplicating Divine confirmations expansion consolidation these territories assuring solid foundation future pillars Universal House of Justice.

[Cablegram, September 1, 1966]*

Vital Needs of the Bahá'í World Center

The time has now come in the progress of the Nine Year Plan when the Bahá'í world must devote a greater effort towards the development of the Faith at its World Center.

Nearly all the accessible unsettled territories of the Plan have now been settled; bases have been established throughout the world for the future expansion of the Faith; a program of progressive consolidation is being pursued hand-in-hand with continued expansion; plans for the construction of the Panama Temple are well advanced; the Ḥaẓíratu'l-Quds, Temple sites, and endowments called for in the Plan are being steadily acquired; by the end of the next Riḍván period eighty-one out of the 108 national spiritual assemblies called for by 1973 will have been established; and the opening of the period of the proclamation of the Faith is fast approaching.

Since the Universal House of Justice came into being in 1963, its primary concern at the World Center of the Faith has been with the basic, minimum essentials of undertaking repairs to the holy places; establishing its administrative offices; reorganizing the accommodation of pilgrims; gathering its staff; developing a suitable housing program for the Hands of the Cause and their families, the members of the House of Justice and their families, and all other believers serving at the World Center; formulating plans for the expansion of the gardens and taking the first steps in their initiation; collating the Sacred Texts and the letters of Shoghi Effendi and indexing them; and fostering relations with the government of the State of Israel and with the United Nations.

The increased burden which these essential steps have imposed upon the International Fund we have endeavored to keep at a minimum so that, in the early stages of the Plan, the maximum resources could be utilized in the teaching work throughout the world.

However, we must now embark upon certain major undertakings vital to the future progress of the Cause. Extensive beautification of the sacred endowments surrounding the holy shrines in Bahjí and Haifa, as well as the site of the future Mashriqu'l-Adhkár on Mount Carmel, must be undertaken, both for its own sake and for the protection of these lands which are situated within the boundaries of rapidly expanding cities; the work of classifying and codifying the Holy Texts must be urgently prosecuted; the arrangements for pilgrimage may have to be greatly expanded to provide for the ever-increasing number of applications from East and West; the intercontinental conferences and the International Convention must be held and paid for; and the auxiliary institutions of the Universal House of Justice must begin to unfold so that the ever-growing and increasingly complex work of the World Center of the Faith may continue to be efficiently discharged. Moreover, the vital assistance given by the International Fund to the work of the Hands of the Cause and national spiritual assemblies must be maintained.

The minimum budget requirements of the International Fund have nearly doubled since 1963, and if in addition we are to be enabled to undertake these developments, a much greater flow of funds will be needed than is now available.

We call upon every national spiritual assembly to consider now the amount that it can allocate as a contribution

Vital Needs of the Bahá'í World Center

to the International Fund in its budget for the coming year. In some cases this may mean that contributions made hitherto will be doubled, trebled, or even more greatly increased. Please write as soon as your decision has been made, and not later than April 21, telling us the estimated amount of your allocation.

This is a vitally important matter, and we shall pray in the holy shrines that the friends throughout the world will respond wholeheartedly to this call.

[March 7, 1967]*

Worldwide Proclamation—A New Dimension

At the conclusion of the third year of the Nine Year Plan we acknowledge with thankful hearts the evidences of Divine favor with which Bahá'u'lláh unfailingly sustains and confirms the dedicated efforts of His servants everywhere, and we unhesitatingly affirm our confidence that the community of the Most Great Name can and will, by its determination and sacrificial efforts, achieve complete victory.

Last year the call was raised for the formation, in 1967, of eleven new national spiritual assemblies. All will be elected during the Riḍván period. We welcome with great joy the National Spiritual Assemblies of the Bahá'ís of Algeria and Tunisia with its seat in Algiers; Cameroon Republic with its seat in Victoria; Swaziland, Lesotho, and Mozambique with its seat in Mbabane; Zambia with its seat in Lusaka; Belize with its seat in Belize; the Leeward, Windward, and Virgin Islands with its seat in Charlotte Amalie; Eastern and Southern Arabia with its seat in Baḥrayn; Laos with its seat in Vientiane; Sikkim with its seat in Gangtok; Taiwan with its seat in Taipeh; the Gilbert and Ellice Islands with its seat in Tarawa. The World Center of the Faith will be represented at each national convention by a Hand of the Cause of God, who will present a message from the Universal House of Justice welcoming the new national community and assigning it its share of the goals of the Nine Year Plan.

VISIBLE ACHIEVEMENTS THROUGHOUT THE WORLD

At this Riḍván eighty-one of the 108 national spiritual assemblies, and more than six thousand of the 13,737 local

Worldwide Proclamation—A New Dimension 103

spiritual assemblies called for by 1973, will have been established; of a required 54,102 localities where Bahá'ís reside, 28,217 are reported; fifteen of the sixty-five national incorporations called for have been achieved; seventeen of fifty-two national Ḥaẓíratu'l-Quds, seven of sixty-two Temple sites, thirteen of fifty-four national endowments, fourteen of thirty-two teaching institutes, have been acquired; of the 973 local incorporations called for in the Plan, 123 have been completed; local Ḥaẓíratu'l-Quds acquired are, twenty-four in India, seventeen in Kenya, nine in Uganda, two in South Africa, two in Turkey, and a number in Congo (Kinshasa), while land for eight others has been acquired in Kenya, for four in Cameroon, for two in Pakistan, and for one in Mauritius; in eight countries local endowments supplementary to those called for in the Plan have been acquired.

Iceland, Korea, Liberia, Luxembourg, and Rhodesia now recognize the Bahá'í marriage certificate; the Dominican Republic, Guyana, Hawaii, Iceland, Italy, Kenya, and Luxembourg recognize Bahá'í holy days. A summer school has been established in Liberia, and one, beyond the requirements of the Plan, in Canada, while land for others has been acquired in Argentina, Ethiopia, and Samoa. Twenty-five new languages have been added to the list of those in which Bahá'í literature is available, bringing the total number to 397. The number of territories now opened to the Faith has reached 311, including the recently settled virgin areas of Chiloé Archipelago, Bonaire, Phoenix Islands, and St. Martin, and two territories in addition to those called for in the Plan, namely Melville Island in Australasia and Montserrat in the Windward Islands.

After protracted frustration the National Spiritual Assembly of Persia has finally gained possession of the historic fortress of C͟hihríq, that bleak and lonely citadel which was the last earthly residence of the blessed Báb, and from which He was led forth to His martyrdom in Tabríz. Realization of the long-sought recognition of the Faith in Italy is a wonderful victory, resulting not only in the incorporation of the National Spiritual Assembly, but also of all local spiritual assemblies in Italy and the ability to establish that National Spiritual Assembly's Publishing Trust. In Iceland the Faith has been recognized as one of the island's religions. This provides not only for incorporation of the Local Spiritual Assembly of Reykjavik, but authorizes the chairman of that Assembly to perform Bahá'í marriages and Bahá'í burials, exempts the Faith from certain taxes, permits the observance of Bahá'í holy days, and paves the way for incorporation of the National Spiritual Assembly of that country when it will be formed. The full number of local spiritual assemblies, groups, and localities called for in the Plan has been established in fifty-three territories and islands under the direction of twenty-six national spiritual assemblies; five territories have formed the required number of local spiritual assemblies and seven have reached the specified number of localities.

Since the call was raised a year ago, international traveling teaching, ranging over the five continents and affecting nearly all national communities, has been undertaken. Seventy-eight projects have been completed in Europe, forty-three in America, twenty-seven in Asia, twenty-five in Australasia, which with those in Africa brings the total number to about two hundred. It is greatly hoped that this stimulating activity, so dear to the beloved Master's heart, will be constantly expanded.

A SPIRITUAL CHARGE NO FORCE CAN RESIST

Sustaining all these visible achievements is a constant activity throughout the world of teaching and administration—a perpetual movement, like the ceaseless surge of the

Worldwide Proclamation—A New Dimension

sea, within the Bahá'í community, which is the real cause of its growth. National and local spiritual assemblies facing difficult problems, devising new plans, shouldering responsibility for a community growing in numbers and consciousness, committees striving to accomplish objectives, Bahá'í youth in eager and dedicated activity, individual Bahá'ís and families making efforts for the Cause, to give the Message, or hold a fireside, these constant services attract the confirmation of Bahá'u'lláh, and the more they are supported by prayers and intense dedication and the more extensive they become, the more they release into the world a spiritual charge which no force on earth can resist, and which must eventually bring about the complete triumph of the Cause. It is this organic vitality of the Faith, so readily felt at the World Center, whose exhilaration we wish every believer to share.

WORLD CENTER TASKS

At the World Center of the Faith codification of the Kitáb-i-Aqdas and collation of other important Texts has continued. Work on the highly important task of formulating the constitution of the Universal House of Justice is well advanced. Development and extension of the gardens surrounding the sacred shrines in both Haifa and Bahjí is continuing. Publication of *The Bahá'í World* Volume XIII has been undertaken. This book covers nine years, from 1954 to 1963, almost the entire period of the Ten Year Crusade, and includes a comprehensive article on the beloved Guardian by Amatu'l-Bahá Rúḥíyyih Khánum. A planned development of relationships with the United Nations is being actively pursued. An important supplementary achievement is the establishment of an international Bahá'í audio-visual center whose function is to provide teaching and deepening aids to all national spiritual assemblies, as well as to store and index audio-visual records.

Service of the Hands of the Cause

Throughout the year the services of the beloved Hands of the Cause have shone with an unfailing light. Their constant encouragement of national spiritual assemblies and of believers everywhere to pursue the goals of the Plan and to obtain a deeper understanding of the true meaning of Bahá'u'lláh's Revelation is contributing in no small measure to the progress of that Plan and must exercise a lasting effect on the development of the Bahá'í community. These few gallant and dedicated believers, whose place in history is forever assured by virtue of their appointment to their high office, are indeed a precious legacy left to us by our beloved Guardian, and as the years go by there is increasingly added to the honor and respect which is their due by reason of their exalted rank, the love and admiration of the friends evoked by their constant services.

In response to special needs two changes have been made in the disposition of the Hands during the year, Hand of the Cause John Robarts returning to the Western Hemisphere with a special assignment to his native Canada, and Hand of the Cause Williams Sears returning to Africa. In addition we are delighted to announce that Hand of the Cause Ṭarázu'lláh Samandarí, whose eyes were blessed by beholding Bahá'u'lláh, will represent the Universal House of Justice at the Intercontinental Conference in Chicago, replacing the late Hand of the Cause Leroy Ioas.

The Panama Temple

In the international sphere the great project of raising the Panama Temple has begun with a choice of a design submitted by Mr. Peter Tillotson, an English architect. Mr.

Robert McLaughlin, sometime member of the National Spiritual Assembly of the United States and Dean Emeritus of the School of Architecture of Princeton University, who served as a member of the technical advisory board for the construction of the interior of the Mother Temple of the West in Wilmette, has been appointed architectural consultant to the Universal House of Justice for the building of the Temple. He and Mr. Tillotson have visited the site together, and are working in close cooperation. Pictures and drawings of the new Temple will be published shortly, and the friends will be kept informed of the progress of construction of this House of Worship "situated between the two great oceans," a location which 'Abdu'l-Bahá indicated would become very important in the future and whence the Teachings, once established, "will unite the East and the West, the North and the South."

PIONEERS STILL URGENTLY NEEDED

The brilliant pioneering feat of the second year of the Plan is beginning to reveal its beneficent effects, but pioneers are still urgently needed and will continue to be needed in all parts of the world for consolidation and development of the Faith in the newly won territories as well as for those resettled during the opening years of the Plan. The immediate requirement is for 209 pioneers to settle in eighty-seven territories named on the attached list, and the call is now raised for the speedy achievement of this task. Service in this highly meritorious field is open to every believer and all those who are moved to respond to this particular call are asked to consult the list of territories and to make their offers to their own National Spiritual Assembly. Full details of the requirements in each territory have been sent to the national spiritual assemblies concerned and to the pioneer committees.

A Strong Home Front—Base for Expansion

The constant need for pioneers no less than the approaching worldwide proclamation render it imperative to pay special attention, in every continent, to the home fronts, for they are the sources of manpower and of administrative experience, the solid bases from which all expansion begins, both at home and abroad. The largest increases in numbers of local spiritual assemblies, of groups, and of believers, are called for on the home fronts, and these tasks must be vigorously pursued. Some national spiritual assemblies have phased these important goals, assigning a specified number for achievement each year, thus insuring a planned and flexible approach to the total requirements. Such a systematic and determined prosecution of the home front goals is highly recommended.

The Bahá'í Fund—Our Honor and Our Challenge

The pressing and ever-growing needs of the Bahá'í Fund are called to the attention of all believers. There are great projects already under way or lying ahead which require very large amounts of money for their realization. The Panama Temple—the first only of the two called for in the Nine Year Plan—the beautification and development of the World Center itself, involving a necessary and inevitable increase in facilities to serve the growing needs of the Faith; support of the vital teaching program in many parts of the world; establishment and development of new national spiritual assemblies—all these urgently require the support of the friends everywhere through sustained and sacrificial contributions. As inflation spreads around the world, the consequent increase in the cost of living is balanced, at least in the more affluent countries, by a corresponding increase in personal incomes. The expenses of the

Bahá'í Fund are inevitably and seriously affected by this inflationary condition which can only be relieved by contributions, both of larger amounts and from a larger number of contributors. The House of Justice believes that the financial needs of the Cause should be met by universal participation in giving and urges national and local spiritual assemblies to pursue this goal with vigor and imagination, recalling to the friends the plea of the beloved Guardian to every believer "unhesitatingly to place, each according to his circumstances, his share on the altar of Bahá'í sacrifice." The fact that only we, the Bahá'ís, can contribute financially to the Cause is both our honor and our challenge.

WORLDWIDE PROCLAMATION BEGINS

As we approach the third phase of the Nine Year Plan there opens before us a prospect of enthralling opportunities such as to thrill the heart of every ardent follower of Bahá'u'lláh. For more than a century we have toiled to teach the Cause; heroic sacrifices, dedicated services, prodigious efforts have been made in order to establish the outposts of the Faith in the chief countries, territories, and islands of the earth and to raise the framework of the Administrative Order around the planet. But the Faith of Bahá'u'lláh remains, as yet, unknown to the generality of men. Now at last, at long last, the worldwide community of the Most Great Name is called upon to launch, on a global scale and to every stratum of human society, an enduring and intensive proclamation of the healing message that the Promised One has come and that the unity and well-being of the human race is the purpose of His Revelation. This long-to-be-sustained campaign, commencing next October in commemoration of the centenary of the sounding of the "opening notes" of Bahá'u'lláh's own Proclamation, and gathering momentum throughout the remainder of the Nine Year Plan, may well become the spearhead of other plans to be launched continually until humanity has recognized and gratefully acclaimed its Redeemer and its Lord.

A hundred years ago Bahá'u'lláh Himself addressed the kings, rulers, religious leaders, and peoples of the world. The Universal House of Justice feels it its bounden duty to bring that Message to the attention of the world's leaders today. It is therefore presenting to them, in the form of a book, the essence of Bahá'u'lláh's announcement. Entitled *The Proclamation of Bahá'u'lláh,* a special edition will be presented to heads of state during the opening of the proclamation period and a general edition will be available to the friends in English, French, German, Italian, and Spanish.

The Hands of the Cause of God, Amatu'l-Bahá Rúḥíyyih Khánum, Ugo Giachery, Ṭarázu'lláh Samandarí, 'Alí-Akbar Furútan, Paul Haney, 'Abú'l-Qásim Faizí, who will represent the Universal House of Justice at the Intercontinental Conferences in October to be held in Panama, Sydney, Chicago, Kampala, Frankfurt, and New Delhi respectively, will gather at the World Center in September, a few days before the Feast of Mashíyyat. The members of the House of Justice will join these Hands in supplication at the Shrine of Bahá'u'lláh in Bahjí and will meet with them for consultation in the Mansion. From that Holy Spot these Hands of the Cause will make a special pilgrimage on behalf of the entire Bahá'í world to Adrianople where the Súriy-i-Mulúk was revealed. One hundred years after the historic event which it is their purpose to commemorate, they will, on September 27, gather in the House of Bahá'u'lláh for prayer and meditation, while the members of the Universal House of Justice will, in the Most Holy Shrine at Bahjí, share in the same commemoration and pray for the success of the conferences and of the proclamation program. The entire Bahá'í world will, between the conferences and Riḍván 1968, commemorate the centenary of the opening of that wonderful period in human history when the clouds of Divine bounty showered in lavish profusion their treasures upon men and the portals of the Kingdom were thrown open, disclosing, to all who had eyes to see, a new heaven and a new earth, and the new Jerusalem coming down from God.

THE INTERCONTINENTAL CONFERENCES

Immediately after the Feast of Mashíyyat the Hands of the Cause will travel from Adrianople to their conferences, each bearing the precious trust of a photograph of the Blessed Beauty, which it will be the privilege of those attending the conferences to view. These distinguished Hands will, on their own behalf, each address the conference which they attend, and will bear a message to each conference from the Universal House of Justice whom they represent.

These six conferences, convened to commemorate the opening of Bahá'u'lláh's own Proclamation and to inaugurate a period of proclamation of His Message by the entire company of His followers, will doubtless demonstrate yet again the spirit of joy which pervades such gatherings of the friends and will reinforce them in their determination to seize whatever means and opportunities they may find to raise the Divine call. Honored by the presence of Hands of the Cause, these conferences, focal points of the love and prayers of the friends everywhere, magnets to attract the spiritual powers which alone can confirm their work, will, it is confidently hoped, be potent sources of unity, spiritual enthusiasm, and realistic planning. National spiritual assemblies are called upon to insure that they are represented at the conference held in their continent so that they may share their plans for proclamation with other national spiritual assemblies as well as discuss with them the remaining goals of the Nine Year Plan.

To all those friends in so many countries, suffering in varying degrees from restrictions and oppression which will either prevent altogether, or greatly inhibit, their public commemorations and subsequent proclamation programs, we send a special message of love and assurance. To them we convey the love and admiration of their fellow believers, who, in gratitude for their greater freedom, are determined to blaze abroad such a proclamation of the Divine Message as may well pave the way for the eventual emancipation of the entire body of the Faith.

PROCLAMATION SUSTAINED BY TEACHING

Worldwide proclamation, the unknown sea on which we must soon sail, will add another dimension to our work, a dimension which will, as it develops, complement and reinforce the twin processes of expansion and consolidation. This pattern of teaching, emerging so soon after the completion of the framework of the Administrative Order, may well be the means of advancing the vital work of consolidation and of rendering more effective the teaching wisdom which has been gained in a hundred years, and more particularly since the beloved Guardian called us to systematic and planned activity. Therefore, in those countries where we are free to publicize our religion, this activity must become part of our regular work, included in budgets, assigned to national and local committees for study and implementation and above all for coordination with the programs operating to achieve the goals of the Nine Year Plan. Every effort of proclamation must be sustained by teaching, particularly locally, where public announcements should be related to such efforts. This coordination is essential, for nothing will be more disheartening than for thousands to hear of the Faith and have nowhere to turn for further information.

THE NATURE OF DEEPENING

The beloved Guardian wrote, "To strive to obtain a more adequate understanding of the significance of Bahá'u'lláh's stupendous Revelation must, it is my unalterable conviction, remain the first obligation and the object of the constant endeavor of each one of its loyal adherents," a statement which places the obligation of deepening in the Cause firmly on every believer. It is therefore upon the nature of deepening, rather than upon the desirability of pursuing it, that we wish to comment.

A detailed and exact knowledge of the present structure of Bahá'í administration, or of the bylaws of national and local spiritual assemblies, or of the many and varied applications of Bahá'í law under the diverse conditions prevailing around the world, while valuable in itself, cannot be regarded as the sort of knowledge primarily intended by deepening. Rather is suggested a clearer apprehension of the purpose of God for man, and particularly of His immediate purpose as revealed and directed by Bahá'u'lláh, a purpose as far removed from current concepts of human well-being and happiness as is possible. We should constantly be on our guard lest the glitter and tinsel of an affluent society should lead us to think that such superficial adjustments to the modern world as are envisioned by humanitarian movements or are publicly proclaimed as the policy of enlightened statesmanship—such as an extension to all members of the human race of the benefits of a high standard of living, of education, medical care, technical knowledge—will of themselves fulfill the glorious mission of Bahá'u'lláh. Far otherwise. These are the things which shall be added unto us once we seek the Kingdom of God, and are not themselves the objectives for which the Báb gave His life, Bahá'u'lláh endured such sufferings as none before Him had even endured, the Master and after Him the Guardian bore their trials and afflictions with such superhuman fortitude. Far deeper and more fundamental was their vision, penetrating to the very purpose of human life. We cannot do better, in this respect, than call to the attention of the friends certain themes pursued by Shoghi Effendi in his trenchant statement "The Goal of a New World Order." "The principle of the oneness of mankind," he writes, "implies an organic change in the structure of present-day society, a change such as the world has not yet experienced." Referring to the ". . . epoch-making changes that constitute the greatest landmarks in the history of human civilization," he states that ". . . they cannot appear, when viewed in their proper perspective, except as subsidiary adjustments preluding that transformation of unparalleled majesty and scope which humanity is in this age bound to undergo." In a later document he refers to the civilization to be established by Bahá'u'lláh as one ". . . with a fullness of life such as the world has never seen nor can as yet conceive."

Dearly-loved friends, this is the theme we must pursue in our efforts to deepen in the Cause. What is Bahá'u'lláh's purpose for the human race? For what ends did He submit to the appalling cruelties and indignities heaped upon Him? What does He mean by "a new race of men"? What are the profound changes which He will bring about? The answers are to be found in the Sacred Writings of our Faith and in their interpretation by 'Abdu'l-Bahá and our beloved Guardian. Let the friends immerse themselves in this ocean, let them organize regular study classes for its constant consideration, and, as reinforcement to their effort, let them remember conscientiously the requirements of daily prayer

Worldwide Proclamation—A New Dimension

and reading of the Word of God enjoined upon all Bahá'ís by Bahá'u'lláh.

Imperative Need to Deepen in the Cause

Such dedicated striving on the part of all the friends to deepen in the Cause becomes imperative with the approach of the proclamation program. As this becomes effective more and more attention will be directed to the claims of Bahá'u'lláh and opposition must be expected. "How great, how very great is the Cause!" wrote the Master. "How very fierce the onslaught of all the peoples and kindreds of the earth. Ere long shall the clamor of the multitude throughout Africa, throughout America, the cry of the European and of the Turk, the groaning of India and China, be heard from far and near. One and all, they shall arise with all their power to resist His Cause. Then shall the knights of the Lord, assisted by His grace from on high, strengthened by faith, aided by the power of understanding, and reinforced by the legions of the Covenant, arise and make manifest the truth of the verse: 'Behold the confusion that hath befallen the tribes of the defeated!' "

Mindful of the countless expressions of divine love found in our Scriptures and aware of the extraordinary nature of the crisis facing humanity, we call the friends to a new realization of the very great things which are expected from us in this Day. We recall that the Blessed Beauty, Bahá'u'lláh, as well as His "Best-Beloved" before Him and 'Abdu'l-Bahá after Him bore Their sufferings in this world in order that mankind might be freed from material fetters and "attain unto true liberty," "might prosper and flourish," "attain unto abiding joy, and be filled with gladness," and we pray that the endeavors of the friends may be the means by which this glory and felicity will speedily come to pass.

[Riḍván 1967]

One Hundred Fiftieth Anniversary of Birth of Bahá'u'lláh

November 12, 1967, will mark the 150th anniversary of Bahá'u'lláh's birth. We call the entire Bahá'í world to joyful celebration, befitting an event so momentous to the fortunes of humanity.

The Universal House of Justice feels that the coincidence of this great occasion with the opening of the proclamation period provides a splendid opportunity for bringing to public attention both the spiritual and social import of the Cause. Not only its message, but the historical fact of a new Revelation, with all its implications of a new and worldwide civilization, should be made clear.

Let the friends not hesitate to welcome to their observances, even to those of a devotional character, the non-Bahá'í public, many of whom may well be attracted by the prayers and expressions of gratitude of the believers, no less than by the exalted tone of passages from Bahá'í Writings.

[June 25, 1967]*

Nature and Purpose of Proclamation

In just over three months the period of the worldwide proclamation of the Faith will be opened at the six intercontinental conferences called to celebrate the centenary of the revelation of the Súriy-i-Mulúk. Those conferences will provide an opportunity for representatives of the national spiritual assemblies to exchange ideas and coordinate plans for the proclamation, which will continue throughout the remaining five and a half years of the Plan.

The stimulating effect of this interchange of ideas will produce greatly increased momentum throughout the world, but inasmuch as many projects must be worked out before that date, we feel a few additional comments on the nature and purpose of proclamation will be helpful now.

Proclamation comprises a number of activities, of which publicity is only one. The Universal House of Justice itself will be conveying the Message of Bahá'u'lláh to the heads of all states, but, in addition to this, one of the most important duties of each national spiritual assembly is to acquaint leaders of thought and prominent men and women in its country with the fundamental aims, the history, and the present status and achievements of the Cause. Such an activity must be carried out with the utmost wisdom, discretion, and dignity. Publicity connected with such approaches must be weighed very carefully, as it may be unwise or discourteous. This is, of course, a long-range program, for such things cannot be rushed, but it must be given constant attention.

Another aspect of proclamation is a series of teaching programs designed to reach every stratum of human society

—programs that should be pursued diligently and wisely, using every available resource.

Publicity itself should be well conceived, dignified, and reverent. A flamboyant approach which may succeed in drawing much initial attention to the Cause may ultimately prove to have produced a revulsion which would require great effort to overcome. The standard of dignity and reverence set by the beloved Guardian should always be upheld, particularly in musical and dramatic items; and photographs of the Master should not be used indiscriminately. This does not mean that activities of the youth, for example, should be stultified; one can be exuberant without being irreverent or undermining the dignity of the Cause.

Every land has its own conditions, thus the kind of proclamation activity to be followed in each country should be decided by its national spiritual assembly. National spiritual assemblies need not follow or copy programs initiated in other countries.

In all proclamation activities, follow-up is of supreme importance. Proclamation, expansion, and consolidation are mutually helpful activities which must be carefully interrelated. In some places it is desirable to open a teaching campaign with publicity—in others it is wiser to establish first a solid local community before publicizing the Faith or encouraging contacts with prominent people. Here, again, wisdom is needed.

We have been elated by the enthusiasm with which the Bahá'í community is preparing for the challenging months and years ahead, and we eagerly await those days but a few short months away which will open a period of such promise for the diffusion of God's Word.

[July 2, 1967]*

The Time Is Ripe

[*Message to the Six Intercontinental Conferences*]

On this, the hundredth anniversary of the sounding in Adrianople of the opening notes of Bahá'u'lláh's Proclamation to the rulers, leaders, and peoples of the world, we recall with profound emotion the circumstances surrounding the Faith of God at that time. In a land, termed by Him the "Land of Mystery," the Bearer of God's Revelation had arisen to carry that Faith a stage further in its divinely ordained destiny.

Internally, the infant Cause of God was convulsed by a crisis from whose shadows emerged the majestic figure of Bahá'u'lláh, the visible Center and Head of a newly established Faith. The first pilgrimages were made to His Residence, a further stage in the transfer of the remains of the Báb was achieved, and above all the first intimations were given of the future station of 'Abdu'l-Bahá as the Center of the Covenant and of the revelation of the new laws for the new Day. Externally, the full significance of the new Revelation was proclaimed by no one less than its Divine Bearer, His followers began openly to identify themselves with the Most Great Name, the independent character of the Faith became established, and its fearless exponents took up their pens in defense of its fair name.

Now, a hundred years later, the friends, gathered in the six intercontinental conferences to commemorate the events of the past, privileged to gaze upon the portrait of their Beloved, must consider the urgent needs of the Cause today.

As the Bahá'í world enters the third phase of the Nine Year Plan we are called upon to proclaim once again that Divine Message to the leaders and masses of the world, to aid the Faith of God to emerge from obscurity into the arena of public attention, to demonstrate through steadfast adherence to its laws the independent character of its mission, and to brace ourselves in preparation for the attacks that are bound to be directed against its victorious onward march. Upon our efforts depends in very large measure the fate of humanity. The hundred years' respite having ended, the struggle between the forces of darkness—man's lower nature—and the rising sun of the Divine Teachings which draw him on to his true station, intensifies day by day.

The centenary campaign has been opened by the Universal House of Justice presenting to 140 heads of state a compilation of Bahá'u'lláh's own Proclamation. The friends must now take the Message to the rest of humanity. The time is ripe and the opportunities illimitable. We are not alone nor helpless. Sustained by our love for each other and given power through the Administrative Order—so laboriously erected by our beloved Guardian—the army of Light can achieve such victories as will astonish posterity.

We pray at the holy shrines that these intercontinental conferences will be centers of spiritual illumination inspiring the friends to redouble their efforts in further expanding and consolidating the Faith of God, to arise to fill the remaining pioneer goals, to undertake traveling teaching projects, and to offer generously of their substance to the various funds, particularly to the vital project of erecting the Panama Temple, the foundation stone of which is being laid by Amatu'l-Bahá Rúḥíyyih Khánum during the course of these conferences.

As humanity enters the dark heart of this age of transition our course is clear—the achievement of the assigned goals and the proclamation of Bahá'u'lláh's healing Message. It is our ardent hope that from these conferences valiant souls may arise with noble resolve and in loving service to ensure the successful and early accomplishment of the sacred tasks that lie ahead.

[October 1967]

Third Phase of Nine Year Plan Begins

Hearts filled profound gratitude rejoice announce inauguration third phase Nine Year Plan through successful consummation six intercontinental conferences attended by 9,200 believers including nearly all Hands Cause large number Board members representatives almost all national assemblies Bahá'í world over 140 territories and host of Asian African American Indian tribes. Inestimable privilege conferred participants through viewing portrait Abhá Beauty. Spirit Holy Land and Adrianople conveyed six distinguished representatives House Justice. First presentations behalf House Justice proclamation book heads of state made before and during conference. Fruitful deliberations held proclamation execution remaining goals Plan. Solidarity Bahá'í world further evinced through ingenious scheme telephonic exchange greetings all six conferences. Spiritual potencies this new phase reinforced through formal laying by Amatu'l-Bahá of cornerstone Mother Temple Latin America. Over 230 offers made at conferences join ranks valiant pioneers Cause. Raise supplicant hands Bahá'u'lláh endow friends every land fresh measure celestial strength enable them pursue with increased vision unabated resolve glorious goals ahead until this new period proclamation yields its share in divinely propelled process establishment Kingdom God hearts men.

[Cablegram, October 15, 1967]

Significant Step at United Nations

Morrow six intercontinental conferences inaugurating proclamation period announce Bahá'í world significant step development relations United Nations through assumption by Universal House of Justice function representation Bahá'í International Community capacity nongovernmental organization at United Nations. Take this occasion express National Assembly United States and Mildred Mottahedeh grateful loving appreciation many years devoted tireless successful services as representative and observer respectively.

[Cablegram, October 17, 1967]

The Paramount Goal of Teaching

We have recently sent to those national spiritual assemblies which are engaged in mass teaching the enclosed extracts from the writings of Bahá'u'lláh and 'Abdu'l-Bahá and from the letters of Shoghi Effendi. We feel that they will also be of great assistance to all other national spiritual assemblies.

The paramount goal of the teaching work at the present time is to carry the Message of Bahá'u'lláh to every stratum of human society and every walk of life. An eager response to the teachings will often be found in the most unexpected quarters, and any such response should be quickly followed up, for success in a fertile area awakens a response in those who were at first uninterested.

The same presentation of the teachings will not appeal to everybody; the method of expression and the approach must be varied in accordance with the outlook and interests of the hearer. An approach which is designed to appeal to everybody will usually result in attracting the middle section, leaving both extremes untouched. No effort must be spared to ensure that the healing Word of God reaches the rich and the poor, the learned and the illiterate, the old and the young, the devout and the atheist, the dweller in the remote hills and islands, the inhabitant of the teeming cities, the suburban businessman, the laborer in the slums, the nomadic tribesman, the farmer, the university student; all must be brought consciously within the teaching plans of the Bahá'í community.

Whereas plans must be carefully made, and every useful

means adopted in the furtherance of this work, your assemblies must never let such plans eclipse the shining truth expounded in the enclosed quotations: that it is the purity of heart, detachment, uprightness, devotion, and love of the teacher that attracts the Divine confirmations and enables him, however ignorant he be in this world's learning, to win the hearts of his fellowmen to the Cause of God.

[October 31, 1967]*

[*Extracts enclosed with above letter*]

"Whoso ariseth, in this Day, to aid Our Cause, and summoneth to his assistance the hosts of a praiseworthy character and upright conduct, the influence flowing from such an action will, most certainly, be diffused throughout the whole world."
(*Gleanings from the Writings of Bahá'u'lláh*, p. 287)

"Whoso ariseth to teach Our Cause must needs detach himself from all earthly things, and regard, at all times, the triumph of Our Faith as his supreme objective. . . . And when he determineth to leave his home, for the sake of the Cause of his Lord, let him put his whole trust in God, as the best provision for his journey, and array himself with the robe of virtue. . . . If he be kindled with the fire of His love, if he forgoeth all created things, the words he uttereth shall set on fire them that hear him."
(*Gleanings from the Writings of Bahá'u'lláh*, pp. 334-335)

"I swear by Him Who is the Most Great Ocean! Within the very breath of such souls as are pure and sanctified far-reaching potentialities are hidden. So great are these potentialities that they exercise their influence upon all created things."

> (*Bahá'u'lláh*—Quoted in *The Advent of Divine Justice,* p. 19)

"He is the true servant of God, who, in this day, were he to pass through cities of silver and gold, would not deign to look upon them, and whose heart would remain pure and undefiled from whatever things can be seen in this world, be they its goods or its treasures. I swear by the Sun of Truth! The breath of such a man is endowed with potency, and his words with attraction."

> (*Bahá'u'lláh*—Quoted in *The Advent of Divine Justice,* p. 19)

"The most vital duty, in this day, is to purify your characters, to correct your manners, and improve your conduct. The beloved of the Merciful must show forth such character and conduct among His creatures that the fragrance of their holiness may be shed upon the whole world, and may quicken the dead, inasmuch as the purpose of the Manifestation of God and the dawning of the limitless lights of the Invisible is to educate the souls of men, and refine the character of every living man."

> (*'Abdu'l-Bahá*—Quoted in *The Advent of Divine Justice,* pp. 21-22)

"If you observe that a soul has turned his face completely toward the Cause of God, his intention is centralized upon the penetration of the Word of God, he is serving the Cause day and night with the utmost fidelity, no scent of selfishness is inhaled from his manners and deeds, and no trace of egotism or prejudice is seen in his personality—nay rather is he a wanderer in the wilderness of the love of God, and one intoxicated with the wine of the knowl-

edge of God, occupied wholly with the diffusion of the fragrances of God, and attracted to the signs of the Kingdom of God; know ye of a certainty that he is confirmed with the powers of the Kingdom, assisted by the heaven of might; and he will shine, gleam, and sparkle like unto the morning star with the utmost brilliancy and splendor from the horizon of the everlasting gift. If he is alloyed with the slightest trace of passion, desire, ostentation, or self-interest, it is certain that the results of all efforts will prove fruitless, and he will become deprived and hopeless.
(*Tablets of 'Abdu'l-Bahá*—Volume I, p. 42)

"The aim is this: the intention of the teacher must be pure, his heart independent, his spirit attracted, his thought at peace, his resolution firm, his magnanimity exalted, and in the love of God a shining torch. Should he become as such, his sanctified breath will even affect the rock; otherwise there will be no result whatsoever. As long as a soul is not perfected, how can he efface the defects of others! Unless he is detached from aught else save God, how can he teach the severance to others!"
(*'Abdu'l-Bahá*—Quoted in *Bahá'í World Faith*, p. 427)

"One thing and only one thing will unfailingly and alone secure the undoubted triumph of this sacred Cause, namely, the extent to which our own inner life and private character mirror forth in their manifold aspects the splendor of those eternal principles proclaimed by Bahá'u'lláh."
(From a letter written by the Guardian to the American believers, dated September 24, 1924, quoted in *Bahá'í Administration*, p. 66)

". . . .having attained sufficiently the individual regeneration—the essential requisite of teaching—let us arise to teach His Cause with righteousness, conviction, understand-

ing, and vigor. Let this be the paramount and most urgent duty of every Bahá'í."
>(From a letter written by the Guardian to the American believers, dated November 24, 1924, quoted in *Bahá'í Administration,* p. 69)

"The first and most important qualification of a Bahá'í teacher is, indeed, unqualified loyalty and attachment to the Cause. Knowledge is, of course, essential; but compared to devotion it is secondary in importance.

"What the Cause now requires is not so much a group of highly cultured and intellectual people who can adequately present its teachings, but a number of devoted, sincere, and loyal supporters who, in utter disregard of their own weaknesses and limitations, and with hearts afire with the love of God, forsake their all for the sake of spreading and establishing His Faith."
>(From a letter written on the Guardian's behalf to an individual believer, published in *Bahá'í News* No. 102, August 1936, p. 2)

"They must remember the glorious history of the Cause, which . . . . was established by dedicated souls who, for the most part, were neither rich, famous, nor well educated, but whose devotion, zeal, and self-sacrifice overcame every obstacle and won miraculous victories for the Faith of God."
>(From a letter written on the Guardian's behalf to the National Spiritual Assembly of India and Burma dated June 29, 1941)

". . . .what raised aloft the banner of Bahá'u'lláh was the love, sacrifice, and devotion of His humble followers and the change that His Teachings wrought in their hearts and lives."
>(From a letter written on the Guardian's behalf to the

British National Spiritual Assembly, dated June 20, 1942)

"It is the quality of devotion and self-sacrifice that brings rewards in the service of this Faith, rather than means, ability, or financial backing."
(From a letter written on the Guardian's behalf to the National Spiritual Assembly of Australia and New Zealand, dated May 11, 1948)

"One wise and dedicated soul can so often give life to an inactive community, bring in new people, and inspire them to greater sacrifice. He hopes that whatever else you are able to do during the coming months, you will be able to keep in circulation a few really good Bahá'í teachers."
(From a letter written on the Guardian's behalf to the National Spiritual Assembly of Central America, dated June 30, 1952)

Convocation of First Oceanic Conference

Occasion hundred fiftieth anniversary Birth Blessed Beauty we contemplate with hearts overflowing gratitude inestimable bounties conferred by God through His Supreme Manifestation ensuring fulfillment glorious long promised Kingdom now evolving womb travailing age destined confer peace undreamt felicity mankind. Announce convocation twenty-third to twenty-fifth August 1968 first Oceanic Conference Bahá'í world Palermo Sicily heart sea traversed God's Manifestation century ago proceeding incarceration Most Great Prison. Twofold purpose conference consider momentous fulfillment age-old prophecies triumph God's Messenger over every grievous calamity and consult plans propagation Cause islands lands bordering Mediterranean Sea. Participants invited Holy Land immediately following conference attend commemoration arrival Lord Hosts these sacred shores reconsecrate themselves Threshold His Shrine prosecution glorious tasks ahead.

[Cablegram, November 12, 1967]

Relationship of Bahá'ís to Politics

[*Portions of a letter written to an individual believer who asked questions about the relationship of Bahá'ís to the social and political forces presently operating in the world.*]

... we will gladly attempt to clarify some of the points which bewilder you in the relationship of Bahá'ís to politics. This is a matter of very great importance, particularly in these days when the world situation is so confused; an unwise act or statement by a Bahá'í in one country could result in a grave setback for the Faith there or elsewhere—and even loss of the lives of fellow believers.

The whole conduct of a Bahá'í in relation to the problems, sufferings, and bewilderment of his fellowmen should be viewed in the light of God's purpose for mankind in this age and the processes He has set in motion for its achievement.

When Bahá'u'lláh proclaimed His Message to the world in the nineteenth century He made it abundantly clear that the first step essential for the peace and progress of mankind was its unification. As He says, "The well-being of mankind, its peace and security are unattainable unless and until its unity is firmly established." (*The World Order of Bahá'u'lláh* p. 203) To this day, however, you will find most people take the opposite point of view: they look upon unity as an ultimate, almost unattainable goal and concentrate first on remedying all the other ills of mankind. If they did but know it, these other ills are but various symptoms and side effects of the basic disease—disunity.

Bahá'u'lláh has, furthermore, stated that the revivification of mankind and the curing of all its ills can be achieved only through the instrumentality of His Faith. "The vitality of men's belief in God is dying out in every land; nothing short of His wholesome medicine can ever restore it. The corrosion of ungodliness is eating into the vitals of human society; what else but the Elixir of His potent Revelation can cleanse and revive it?" (*Gleanings from the Writings of Bahá'u'lláh*, XCIX) "That which the Lord hath ordained as the sovereign remedy and mightiest instrument for the healing of all the world is the union of all its peoples in one universal Cause, one common Faith. This can in no wise be achieved except through the power of a skilled, an all-powerful and inspired Physician. This, verily, is the truth, and all else naught but error." (*Gleanings from the Writings of Bahá'u'lláh*, CXX)

The Impotence of Statesmanship

In similar vein the beloved Guardian wrote: "Humanity, whether viewed in the light of man's individual conduct or in the existing relationships between organized communities and nations, has, alas, strayed too far and suffered too great a decline to be redeemed through the unaided efforts of the best among its recognized rulers and statesmen —however disinterested their motives, however concerted their action, however unsparing in their zeal and devotion to its cause. No scheme which the calculations of the highest statesmanship may yet devise; no doctrine which the most distinguished exponents of economic theory may hope to advance; no principle which the most ardent of moralists may strive to inculcate, can provide, in the last resort, adequate foundations upon which the future of a distracted world can be built.

"No appeal for mutual tolerance which the worldly-wise

might raise, however compelling and insistent, can calm its passions or help restore its vigor. Nor would any general scheme of mere organized international cooperation, in whatever sphere of human activity, however ingenious in conception, or extensive in scope, succeed in removing the root cause of the evil that has so rudely upset the equilibrium of present-day society. Not even, I venture to assert, would the very act of devising the machinery required for the political and economic unification of the world—a principle that has been increasingly advocated in recent times —provide in itself the antidote against the poison that is steadily undermining the vigor of organized peoples and nations.

"What else, might we not confidently affirm, but the unreserved acceptance of the Divine program enunciated, with such simplicity and force as far back as sixty years ago, by Bahá'u'lláh, embodying in its essentials God's divinely appointed scheme for the unification of mankind in this age, coupled with an indomitable conviction in the unfailing efficacy of each and all of its provisions, is eventually capable of withstanding the forces of internal disintegration which, if unchecked, must needs continue to eat into the vitals of a despairing society." (*The World Order of Bahá'u'lláh*, pp. 33, 34)

Two Great Processes at Work

We are told by Shoghi Effendi that two great processes are at work in the world: the great Plan of God, tumultuous in its progress, working through mankind as a whole, tearing down barriers to world unity and forging humankind into a unified body in the fires of suffering and experience. This process will produce, in God's due time, the Lesser Peace, the political unification of the world. Mankind at that time can be likened to a body that is unified but without life. The second process, the task of breathing life into this unified body—of creating true unity and spirituality culminating in the Most Great Peace—is that of the Bahá'ís, who are laboring consciously, with detailed instructions and continuing Divine guidance, to erect the fabric of the Kingdom of God on earth, into which they call their fellowmen, thus conferring upon them eternal life.

The working out of God's Major Plan proceeds mysteriously in ways directed by Him alone, but the Minor Plan that He has given us to execute, as our part in His grand design for the redemption of mankind, is clearly delineated. It is to this work that we must devote all our energies, for there is no one else to do it. So vital is this function of the Bahá'ís that Bahá'u'lláh has written: "O friends! Be not careless of the virtues with which ye have been endowed, neither be neglectful of your high destiny. Suffer not your labors to be wasted through the vain imaginations which certain hearts have devised. Ye are the stars of the heaven of understanding, the breeze that stirreth at the break of day, the soft-flowing waters upon which must depend the very life of all men, the letters inscribed upon His sacred scroll. With the utmost unity, and in a spirit of perfect fellowship, exert yourselves, that ye may be enabled to achieve that which beseemeth this Day of God." (*Gleanings from the Writings of Bahá'u'lláh*, XCVI)

THE MOST IMPORTANT TASKS

Because love for our fellowmen and anguish at their plight are essential parts of a true Bahá'í's life, we are continually drawn to do what we can to help them. It is vitally important that we do so whenever the occasion presents itself, for our actions must say the same thing as our words —but this compassion for our fellows must not be allowed to divert our energies into channels which are ultimately doomed to failure, causing us to neglect the most important and fundamental work of all. There are hundreds of thousands of well-wishers of mankind who devote their lives to works of relief and charity, but a pitiful few to do the work which God Himself most wants done: the spiritual awakening and regeneration of mankind.

It is often through our misguided feeling that we can somehow aid our fellows better by some activity outside the Faith, that Bahá'ís are led to indulge in politics. This is a dangerous delusion. As Shoghi Effendi's secretary wrote on his behalf: "What we Bahá'ís must face is the fact that society is disintegrating so rapidly that moral issues which were clear a half century ago are now hopelessly confused and, what is more, thoroughly mixed up with battling political interests. That is why the Bahá'ís must turn all their forces into the channel of building up the Bahá'í Cause and its administration. They can neither change nor help the world in any other way at present. If they become involved in the issues the governments of the world are struggling over, they will be lost. But if they build up the Bahá'í pattern they can offer it as a remedy when all else has failed." (*Bahá'í News* No. 241, March 1951, p. 14) ". . . We must build up our Bahá'í system, and leave the faulty systems of the world to go their way. We cannot change them through becoming involved in them; on the contrary, they will destroy us." (*Bahá'í News* No. 215, January 1949, p. 1)

Other instructions from the Guardian, covering the same theme in more detail, can be found on pages 24 and 29 to 32 of *Principles of Bahá'í Administration* (1963 edition); you are no doubt already familiar with these.

The key to a true understanding of these principles seems to be in these words of Bahá'u'lláh: "O people of God! Do not busy yourselves in your own concerns; let your thoughts be fixed upon that which will rehabilitate the fortunes of mankind and sanctify the hearts and souls of men. This can best be achieved through pure and holy deeds, through a virtuous life and a goodly behavior. Valiant acts will ensure the triumph of this Cause, and a saintly character will reinforce its power. Cleave unto righteousness, O people of Bahá! This, verily, is the commandment which this wronged One hath given unto you, and the first choice of His unrestrained will for every one of you." (*Gleanings from the Writings of Bahá'u'lláh*, XLIII)

[December 8, 1967]

Newly Elected Universal House of Justice

Announce Bahá'í world newly elected members Universal House of Justice Amoz Gibson 'Alí Nakhjavání Hushmand Fatheázam Ian Semple Charles Wolcott David Hofman H. Borrah Kavelin Hugh Chance David Ruhe.

[Cablegram, April 22, 1968]

Message to National Conventions—1968

With joyful memory of dedicated spirit mature deliberations second International Convention hail golden opportunity national conventions as crucial midway point Nine Year Plan approaches galvanize believers direct all efforts achievement every remaining goal and simultaneously extend accelerate universal proclamation Divine Message. With utmost love call upon all Bahá'ís for sacrificial outpouring energies resources advancement redeeming Order Bahá'u'lláh sole refuge misdirected heedless millions. World Center Faith scene prolonged prayerful consultation with assembled Hands Cause goals Plan including fundamental objective development institution Hands view extension future God-given duties protection propagation. Supplicating continually Holy Shrines Lord Hosts bountifully reward dedicated ardent lovers complete glorious victory.

[Cablegram, May 9, 1968]

Continental Boards of Counselors Established

Rejoice announce momentous decision establish eleven Continental Boards Counselors protection propagation Faith three each for Africa Americas Asia one each for Australasia Europe. Adoption this significant step following consultation with Hands Cause God ensures extension future appointed functions their institution. Continental Boards entrusted in close collaboration Hands Cause with responsibility direction Auxiliary Boards and consultation national spiritual assemblies. Hands Cause God will henceforth increase intercontinental services assuming worldwide role protection propagation Faith. Members Auxiliary Boards will report be responsible to Continental Boards Counselors. Hands Cause residing Holy Land in addition serving liaison between Universal House Justice and Continental Boards Counselors will assist future establishment international teaching center Holy Land foreshadowed writings beloved Guardian. Details new developments being conveyed by letter. Fervently supplicating Holy Threshold Divine confirmations further step irresistible unfoldment mighty Administrative Order Bahá'u'lláh.

[Cablegram, June 21, 1968]*

Appointment of Continental Boards of Counselors

The majestic unfoldment of Bahá'u'lláh's world-redeeming administrative system has been marked by the successive establishment of the various institutions and agencies which constitute the framework of that divinely created Order. Thus, more than a quarter of a century after the emergence of the first national spiritual assemblies of the Bahá'í world the institution of the Hands of the Cause of God was formally established, with the appointment by the beloved Guardian, in conformity with the provisions of 'Abdu'l-Bahá's Will and Testament, of the first contingent of these high-ranking officers of the Faith. Following the passing of the Guardian of the Cause of God, it fell to the House of Justice to devise a way, within the Administrative Order, of developing "the institution of the Hands of the Cause with a view to extension into the future of its appointed functions of protection and propagation," and this was made a goal of the Nine Year Plan. Much thought and study has been given to the question over the past four years, and the texts have been collected and reviewed. During the last two months, this goal, as announced in our cable to the national conventions, has been the object of prolonged and prayerful consultation between the Universal House of Justice and the Hands of the Cause of God. All this made evident the framework within which this goal was to be achieved, namely:

> The Universal House of Justice sees no way in which additional Hands of the Cause of God can be appointed.

The absence of the Guardian of the Faith brought about an entirely new relationship between the Universal House of Justice and the Hands of the Cause and called for the progressive unfoldment by the Universal House of Justice of the manner in which the Hands of the Cause would carry out their divinely conferred functions of protection and propagation.

Whatever new development or institution is initiated should come into operation as soon as possible in order to reinforce and supplement the work of the Hands of the Cause while at the same time taking full advantage of the opportunity of having the Hands themselves assist in launching and guiding the new procedures.

Any such institution must grow and operate in harmony with the principles governing the functioning of the institution of the Hands of the Cause of God.

In the light of these considerations the Universal House of Justice decided, as announced in its recent cable, to establish Continental Boards of Counselors for the protection and propagation of the Faith. Their duties will include directing the Auxiliary Boards in their respective areas, consulting and collaborating with national spiritual assemblies, and keeping the Hands of the Cause and the Universal House of Justice informed concerning the conditions of the Cause in their areas.

Initially eleven Boards of Counselors have been appointed, one for each of the following areas: Northwestern Africa, Central and East Africa, Southern Africa, North America, Central America, South America, Western Asia, Southeastern Asia, Northeastern Asia, Australasia, and Europe.

The members of these Boards of Counselors will serve for a term, or terms, the length of which will be determined and announced at a later date, and while serving in this capacity will not be eligible for membership on national or local administrative bodies. One member of each Continental Board of Counselors has been designated as trustee of the Continental Fund for its area.

The Auxiliary Boards for Protection and Propagation will henceforth report to the Continental Boards of Counselors, who will appoint or replace members of the Auxiliary Boards as circumstances may require. Such appointments and replacements as may be necessary in the initial stages will take place after consultation with the Hand or Hands previously assigned to the continent or zone.

The Hands of the Cause of God have the prerogative and obligation to consult with the Continental Boards of Counselors and national spiritual assemblies on any subject which, in their view, affects the interests of the Cause. The Hands residing in the Holy Land will act as liaison between the Universal House of Justice and the Continental Boards of Counselors, and will also assist the Universal House of Justice in setting up, at a propitious time, an international teaching center in the Holy Land, as anticipated in the Guardian's writings.

The Hands of the Cause of God are one of the most precious assets the Bahá'í world possesses. Released from administration of the Auxiliary Boards, they will be able to concentrate their energies on the more primary responsibilities of general protection and propagation, "preservation of the spiritual health of the Bahá'í communities" and "the vitality of the faith" of the Bahá'ís throughout the world. The House of Justice will call upon them to undertake special missions on its behalf, to represent it on both Bahá'í and other occasions, and to keep it informed of the welfare of the Cause. While the Hands of the Cause will, naturally, have special concern for the affairs of the Cause

Appointment of Continental Boards of Counselors 143

in the areas in which they reside, they will operate increasingly on an intercontinental level, a factor which will lend tremendous impetus to the diffusion throughout the Bahá'í world of the spiritual inspiration channeled through them —the Chief Stewards of Bahá'u'lláh's embryonic World Commonwealth.

With joyful hearts we proclaim this further unfoldment of the Administrative Order of Bahá'u'lláh and join our prayers to those of the friends throughout the East and the West that Bahá'u'lláh may continue to shower His confirmations upon the efforts of His servants in the safeguarding and promotion of His Faith.

[June 24, 1968]

[*Membership of First Continental Boards of Counselors*]

The Universal House of Justice has announced the names of those who have been appointed to the first Continental Boards of Counselors for the Protection and Propagation of the Faith as follows:

NORTHWESTERN AFRICA
 Ḥusayn Ardikání (Trustee, Continental Fund), Muḥammad Kebdani, William Maxwell.
CENTRAL AND EAST AFRICA
 Oloro Epyeru, Kolonario Oule, Isobel Sabri, Mihdí Samandarí, 'Azíz Yazdí (Trustee, Continental Fund).
SOUTHERN AFRICA
 Seewoosumbur-Jeehoba Appa, Shidán Fatḥ-i-A'ẓam (Trustee, Continental Fund), Bahíyyih Ford.
NORTH AMERICA
 Lloyd Gardiner, Florence Mayberry, Edna True (Trustee, Continental Fund).

CENTRAL AMERICA
  Carmen de Burafato, Artemus Lamb, Alfred Osborne (Trustee, Continental Fund).
SOUTH AMERICA
  Athos Costas, Hooper Dunbar (Trustee, Continental Fund), Donald Witzel.
WESTERN ASIA
  Masíh Farhangí, Mas'úd Khamsí, Hádí Rahmání (Trustee, Continental Fund), Manúchihr Salmánpúr, Sankaran-Nair Vasudevan.
SOUTHEAST ASIA
  Yan Kee Leong, Khudárahm Paymán (Trustee, Continental Fund), Chellie Sundram.
NORTHEAST ASIA
  Rúhu'lláh Mumtází (Trustee, Continental Fund), Vicente Samaniego.
AUSTRALASIA
  Suhayl 'Alá'í, Howard Harwood, Thelma Perks (Trustee, Continental Fund).
EUROPE
  Erik Blumenthal, Dorothy Ferraby (Trustee, Continental Fund), Louis Hénuzet.

From Gallipoli to the Most Great Prison

[*Message to First Oceanic Conference*]

The event which we commemorate at this first Bahá'í Oceanic Conference is unique. Neither the migration of Abraham from Ur of the Chaldees to the region of Aleppo, nor the journey of Moses towards the Promised Land, nor the flight into Egypt of Mary and Joseph with the infant Jesus, nor yet the Hegira of Muḥammad can compare with the voyage made by God's Supreme Manifestation one hundred years ago from Gallipoli to the Most Great Prison. Bahá'u'lláh's voyage was forced upon Him by the two despots who were His chief adversaries in a determined attempt to extirpate once and for all His Cause, and the decree of His fourth banishment came when the tide of His prophetic utterance was in full flood. The Proclamation of His Message to mankind had begun; the sun of His majesty had reached its zenith and, as attested by the devotion of His followers, the respect of the population, and the esteem of officials and the representatives of foreign powers, His ascendancy had become manifest. At such a time He was confronted with the decree of final exile to a remote, obscure, and pestilential outpost of the decrepit Turkish empire.

Bahá'u'lláh knew, better than His royal persecutors, the magnitude of the crisis, with all its potentiality for disaster, which confronted Him. Consigned to a prison cell, debarred from access to those to whom His Message must be addressed, cut off from His followers save for the handful who were to accompany Him, and deprived even of association with them, it was apparent that by all earthly standards the ship of His Cause must founder, His mission wither and die.

But it was the Lord of Hosts with Whom they were dealing. Knowing the sufferings which faced Him, His one thought was to instill confidence and fortitude into His followers, to whom He immediately despatched sublime Tablets asserting the power of His Cause to overcome all opposition. "Should they attempt to conceal its light on the continent," is one of His powerful utterances on this theme, "it will assuredly rear its head in the midmost heart of the ocean, and raising its voice, proclaim: 'I am the lifegiver of the world!'" All the afflictions which men could heap upon Him were thrown back from the rock of His adamantine will like spray from the ocean. His patient submission to the affronts of men, His fortitude, His divine genius transformed the somber notes of disaster into the diapason of triumph. At the nadir of His worldly fortunes He raised His standard of victory above the Prison City and poured forth upon mankind the healing balm of His laws and ordinances revealed in His Most Holy Book. "Until our time," comments 'Abdu'l-Bahá, "no such thing has ever occurred."

THE PART WE MUST PLAY

Contemplating this awe-inspiring, supernal episode, we may obtain a clearer understanding of our own times, a more confident view of their outcome, and a deeper apprehension of the part we are called upon to play. That the violent disruption which has seized the entire planet is beyond the ability of men to assuage, unaided by God's Revelation, is a truth repeatedly and forcibly set forth in our Writings. The old order cannot be repaired; it is being rolled up before our eyes. The moral decay and disorder convulsing human society must run their course; we can neither arrest nor divert them.

Our task is to build the Order of Bahá'u'lláh. Undeflected by the desperate expedients of those who seek to subdue the storm convulsing human life by political, economic, social, or educational programs, let us, with single-minded devotion and concentrating all our efforts on our objective, raise His Divine system and, sheltered within its impregnable stronghold, safe from the darts of doubtfulness, demonstrate the Bahá'í way of life. Wherever a Bahá'í community exists, whether large or small, let it be distinguished for its abiding sense of security and faith, its high standard of rectitude, its complete freedom from all forms of prejudice, the spirit of love among its members, and for the closely knit fabric of its social life. The acute distinction between this and present-day society will inevitably arouse the interest of the more enlightened, and as the world's gloom deepens the light of Bahá'í life will shine brighter and brighter until its brilliance must eventually attract the disillusioned masses and cause them to enter the haven of the Covenant of Bahá'u'lláh, Who alone can bring them peace and justice and an ordered life.

BEFITTING SCENE FOR FIRST OCEANIC CONFERENCE

The great sea, on one of whose chief islands you are now gathered, within whose hinterland and islands have flourished the Jewish, the Christian, and Islamic civilizations, is a befitting scene for the first Oceanic Bahá'í Conference. Two milleniums ago, in this arena, the disciples of Christ performed such deeds of heroism and self-sacrifice as are remembered to this day and are forever enshrined in the annals of His Cause. A thousand years later the lands bordering the southern and western shores of this sea witnessed the glory of Islám's Golden Age.

In the day of the Promised One this same sea achieved eternal fame through its association with the Heroic and Formative Ages of His Cause. It bore upon its bosom the King of Kings Himself; the Center of His Covenant crossed and recrossed it in the course of His epoch-making journeys to the West, during which He left the indelible imprint of His presence upon European and African lands; the Sign of God on earth frequently journeyed upon it. It enshrines within its depths the mortal remains of the Hand of the Cause of God Dorothy Baker, and around its shores lies the dust of apostles, martyrs, and pioneers. Forty-six Knights of Bahá'u'lláh are identified with seven of its islands and five of its territories. Through such and many other episodes, Mediterranean lands—ancient home of civilizations—have been endowed with spiritual potentiality to dissolve the encrustations of those once glorious but now moribund social orders and to radiate once again the light of Divine guidance.

Through dedicated, heroic, and sacrificial deeds during the course of the beloved Guardian's ministry, the Faith of Bahá'u'lláh was established in this area. Eight pillars of the Universal House of Justice were raised, the first of an even larger number to be established now and during the course of future plans, to include, as envisioned by Shoghi Effendi, national spiritual assemblies in major islands of that historic sea.

ENGENDER DYNAMIC FOR OVERWHELMING VICTORY

The timing of such exciting developments is dependent upon the outcome of the Nine Year Plan. At this midway point of that Plan, although great strides have been made, more than half the goals are still to be won. The greatest deficiencies are in the opening of new centers where Bahá'ís reside and the formation of local spiritual assemblies, which inevitably affects the ability to establish national spiritual assemblies. A dramatic upsurge of teaching —effective teaching—is necessary to make up the leeway; pioneers are needed, teachers must travel, funds must be provided. It is our hope that there will be engendered at this conference, through your enthusiasm, prayers, and spirit of devotion, a great spiritual dynamic to reinforce that grand momentum which, mounting steadily during the next four years, must carry the community of the Most Great Name to overwhelming victory in 1973.

Dear friends; within a few short days the observance of the Centenary of Bahá'u'lláh's arrival in the Holy Land will take place. The hearts and minds of the entire Bahá'í world will be focused on the Most Holy Shrine, where those privileged to attend this commemoration will circumambulate that Holy Spot and raise their prayers to the Lord of the Age. Let them remember their fellow believers at home and supplicate from the depths of their souls for such bounties and favors to descend upon the friends of God everywhere as to cause them to rise as one man to demonstrate their love for Him Who suffered for them, by such deeds of sacrifice and devotion as shall outshine the deeds of the past and sweep away every obstacle from the onward march of the Cause of God.

[August 1968]

All May Share Laurels of Accomplishment

The glorious conference in Palermo concluded with a burst of eager enthusiasm of determined and dedicated believers who have pledged to do their part in winning the remaining goals of the Nine Year Plan. More than 125 offered to pioneer and more than 100 volunteered to do travel teaching. In addition, there was a generous outpouring of material resources to finance teaching projects. Had the entire Bahá'í world been able to participate in the Mediterranean conference. we have no doubt that all the goals would be quickly won.

With this in mind, we wish to impress upon the friends who could not attend the conference, and who will surely —through reports and personal contact with those who did —sense the enthusiasm generated there, that all believers have the privilege to share in the pioneering work, in the travel teaching program, and in contributing to the Fund.

We announced at the conference that the International Deputization Fund, so far used to aid pioneering and travel teaching on an international level, will henceforth be available to assist such projects on the national level in those areas where support is vitally important to the winning of the goals of the Nine Year Plan. We are concerned that, although we are now approaching the midway point of the Plan, we must yet form an additional 6,997 local spiritual assemblies (76% of the goal), and take the Faith to over 22,800 new localities (59% of the goal). Obviously, hundreds of pioneers and traveling teachers will be required, many of whom will serve in their own countries.

All May Share Laurels of Accomplishment 151

Those who cannot pioneer or do travel teaching will want to participate by contributing to the International Deputization Fund. Let them remember Bahá'u'lláh's injunction: "Center your energies in the propagation of the Faith of God. Whoso is worthy of so high a calling, let him arise and promote it. Whoso is unable, it is his duty to appoint him who will, in his stead, proclaim this Revelation . . ." Let the Bahá'ís of the world join in the true spirit of universal participation and win all the victories while there is yet time. Let each assume his full measure of responsibility that all may share the laurels of accomplishment at the end of the Plan.

Our fervent prayer is that this one hundredth anniversary of the final banishment of Bahá'u'lláh will mark a significant turning point in the fortunes of the Nine Year Plan.

[September 8, 1968]

Pathway of Service for Bahá'í Youth in Every Land

In the two years since we last addressed the youth of the Bahá'í world many remarkable advances have been made in the fortunes of the Faith. Not the least of these is the enrollment under the banner of Bahá'u'lláh of a growing army of young men and women eager to serve His Cause. The zeal, the enthusiasm, the steadfastness, and the devotion of the youth in every land have brought great joy and assurance to our hearts.

During the last days of August and the first days of September, when nearly two thousand believers from all over the world gathered in the Holy Land to commemorate the Centenary of Bahá'u'lláh's arrival on these sacred shores, we had an opportunity to observe at first hand those qualities of good character, selfless service, and determined effort exemplified in the youth who served as volunteer helpers, and we wish to express our gratitude for their loving assistance and for their example.

Many of them offered to pioneer, but one perplexing question recurred: Shall I continue my education, or should I pioneer now? Undoubtedly this same question is in the mind of every young Bahá'í wishing to dedicate his life to the advancement of the Faith. There is no stock answer which applies to all situations; the beloved Guardian gave different answers to different individuals on this question. Obviously circumstances vary with each individual case. Each individual must decide how he can best serve the Cause. In making this decision, it will be helpful to weigh the following factors:

Service for Bahá'í Youth in Every Land

Upon becoming a Bahá'í one's whole life is, or should become, devoted to the progress of the Cause of God, and every talent or faculty he possesses is ultimately committed to this overriding life objective. Within this framework he must consider, among other things, whether by continuing his education now he can be a more effective pioneer later, or alternatively whether the urgent need for pioneers, while possibilities for teaching are still open, outweighs an anticipated increase in effectiveness. This is not an easy decision, since oftentimes the spirit which prompts the pioneering offer is more important than one's academic attainments.

One's liability for military service may be a factor in timing the offer of pioneer service.

One may have outstanding obligations to others, including those who may be dependent on one for support.

It may be possible to combine a pioneer project with a continuing educational program. Consideration may also be given to the possibility that a pioneering experience, even though it interrupts the formal educational program, may prove beneficial in the long run in that studies would later be resumed with a more mature outlook.

The urgency of a particular goal which one is especially qualified to fill and for which there are no other offers.

The fact that the need for pioneers will undoubtedly be with us for many generations to come, and that therefore there will be many calls in future for pioneering service.

The principle of consultation also applies. One may have the obligation to consult others, such as one's parents, one's local and national assemblies, and the pioneering committees.

Finally, bearing in mind the principle of sacrificial service and the unfailing promises Bahá'u'lláh ordained for those who arise to serve His Cause, one should pray and meditate on what one's course of action will be. Indeed, it often happens that the answer will be found in no other way.

We assure the youth that we are mindful of the many important decisions they must make as they tread the path of service to Bahá'u'lláh. We will offer our ardent supplications at the Holy Threshold that all will be divinely guided and that they will attract the blessings of the All-Merciful.

[October 9, 1968]

In Memoriam

In Memoriam

[Hand of the Cause of God Leroy Ioas]

Grieve announce passing outstanding Hand Cause Leroy Ioas. His long service Bahá'í Community United States crowned elevation rank Hand Faith paving way historic distinguished services Holy Land. Appointment first Secretary General International Bahá'í Council personal representative Guardian Faith two intercontinental conferences association his name by beloved Guardian octagon door Báb's Shrine tribute supervisory work drum dome that Holy Sepulcher notable part erection International Archives building all ensure his name immortal annals Faith. Laid to rest Bahá'í cemetery close fellow Hands advise hold befitting memorial services.

[Cablegram, July 22, 1965]

[Hand of the Cause of God Hermann Grossmann]

Deeply regret announce passing Hand Cause Hermann Grossmann. Greatly admired beloved Guardian his grievous loss deprives company Hands Cause outstanding collaborator and Bahá'í world community staunch defender promoter Faith. His courageous loyalty during challenging years tests persecutions Germany outstanding services South America immortalized annals Faith. Invite all national spiritual assemblies hold memorial gatherings befitting his exalted rank exemplary services. Request those responsible Mother Temples arrange services auditorium.

[Cablegram, July 9, 1968]

[*Luṭfu'lláh Ḥakím*]

Following cable sent National Spiritual Assembly Persia "Grieve announce passing Luṭfu'lláh Ḥakím dedicated servant Cause God. Special missions entrusted him full confidence reposed in him by Master and Guardian his close association with early distinguished believers East West including his collaboration Esslemont his services Persia British Isles Holy Land his membership appointed and elected International Bahá'í Council his election Universal House Justice will always be remembered immortal annals Faith Bahá'u'lláh. Inform believers hold befitting memorial meetings all centers. Convey all members his family expressions loving sympathy assurance prayers progress his radiant soul Abhá Kingdom." Request hold memorial gathering Mother Temple West.

[Cablegram, August 12, 1968]

[*Hand of the Cause of God Ṭarázu'lláh Samandarí*]

Have cabled NSA Persia "With sorrowful hearts announce passing Hand Cause God shield His Faith dearly loved Ṭarázu'lláh Samandarí ninety-third year his life on morrow commemoration Centenary Bahá'u'lláh's arrival Holy Land. Faithful to last breath instructions his Lord his Master his Guardian he continued selfless devoted service unabated until falling ill during recent teaching mission. Unmindful illness he proceeded Holy Land participate centenary. Ever remembered hearts believers East West to whose lands he traveled bearing message his Lord whose communities he faithfully served this precious remnant Heroic Age who attained presence Blessed Beauty year His ascension now laid rest foot Mountain God amidst throng believers assembled vicinity very spot Bahá'u'lláh first trod these sacred shores. Request all national assemblies hold memorial services including four Mother Temples Bahá'í world befitting long life dedicated exemplary service Lord Hosts by one assured Center Covenant loving welcome presence Bahá'u'lláh Abhá Kingdom. Extend loving sympathy assurance prayers members distinguished family." Please hold memorial services as requested.

[Cablegram, September 3, 1968]